After the Gospels

After the
Gospels

*Readings from great Christians
of the early Church*

✣

David
Winter

Published by
BRF
First Floor, Elsfield Hall,
15–17 Elsfield Way, Oxford OX2 8FG
ISBN 1 84101 197 5

First published 2001
10 9 8 7 6 5 4 3 2 1 0

A catalogue record for this book is available from the British Library

Printed and bound in Great Britain by
Omnia Books Limited, Glasgow

Contents

Introduction

Probably less than a hundred years after the death of Jesus, the last words of the New Testament as we know it were written—perhaps the mysterious book of the Revelation of John, or possibly the second letter of Peter. What comes as a surprise to many people, including many devout readers of the Bible, is that what we find in its pages is only a part of an enormous literature produced by the first Christians and their leaders. The Gospels and what we call the 'Epistles'—the letters of Paul, Peter, John, James and the others—are simply those writings from the early days of Christianity which were judged by the Church to have 'apostolic' authority: written by, or reflecting very closely, the teaching of the chosen 'first messengers' of Jesus Christ.

But when the last full stop was put on the end of Revelation, or whatever, there was no stop to the literary output of this dynamic new movement. Its bishops still went on writing letters to their churches, its teachers still set out to capture and pass on the essence of the teaching of Jesus and the apostles, its preachers still poured out a stream of exhortation, advice and admonition. Any theological library will show the extent of their output—far exceeding in quantity those writings later given the cachet of being designated the 'Christian Scriptures'.

In recent years, various attempts have been made to exploit these writings in a sensational way—to suggest that there were 'hidden' or 'suppressed' gospels, for instance, offering a very different picture of Jesus and his teaching from the orthodox model. There have been allegations of plots by the leaders of the 'orthodox' party to eliminate any versions of the Jesus story but their own. And, of course, on the back of this have come any number of ludicrous fantasies—such ideas as that Jesus recovered from crucifixion, married Mary Magdalene and escaped to Spain or the south of France to raise a family. In the modern world, no conspiracy theory is ever too bizarre to find a publisher—or an eager audience, apparently.

This book offers none! But what it does do is to introduce the reader to this rich and wonderful tapestry of writing from the first centuries of the Christian Church. After all, no present-day Christian can deny that it is that Church which is the 'mother of us all', whatever our modern labels. Long before there were Episcopalians and Presbyterians, Baptists or Reformed, or even (in the technical sense) Orthodox or Catholic, there was this lively, argumentative, passionate movement which came to be known as the Church of Christ. It was founded on the teaching of the apostles, 'Jesus Christ himself' (they claimed) 'being the chief corner stone'. To meet these first Christians and to reflect on their words is a challenging, exciting and sometimes disturbing experience.

There is, however, another reason for making their writings available to a wider readership, and that is the light they shed on the New Testament itself. After all, the Gospels and the Epistles didn't drop from angelic hands in heaven. They were produced by flesh-and-blood human beings, leaders of the Church, for the benefit of other flesh-and-blood human beings, its members. They are rooted in the soil of the first century and nourished by the developing life of the rapidly growing Church. One of the reasons they seem difficult and even obscure to some modern readers is our assumption that they are 'timeless' (in the sense of being detached from normal constraints of culture, language, idiom and so on). In fact, they are very much products of the moment, often dashed off at white heat to meet an immediate and pressing need—think of Paul's letter to the Galatians! The writers of these letters were not consciously writing for 'posterity', largely because most of them

8

didn't believe there was going to be any—the *parousia*, the appearing of Christ at the Day of the Lord, was expected at any moment.

In fact, of course, they were to be the first and formative voices of a religious movement that would rewrite the history of the world. But *they* didn't know that. We owe it to the providence of God that they produced between them a collection of writings which have served to shape that body, the Christian Church, and provide it with a normative core of teaching and pastoral wisdom. In due course, and after several centuries of agonized debate and reflection, the Church decreed that their writings, what we now call the 'New Testament', were part of the inspired Word of God, on a par, at least, with the Hebrew Scriptures. It was this decision which earned them a special and unique place in the Church's life.

The writings included in this book are *not* part of the Christian Scriptures, so I suppose readers are at liberty to disagree with their contents if they so desire! But they are part of the historical setting of the apostolic writings, or at any rate the decades immediately following, and so may be considered as extremely valuable interpreters of those writings, uniquely able to provide us with a picture of the life and world of the early Church. It seems to me that many of the less edifying arguments about the interpretation of some parts of the New Testament could have been avoided with greater openness to the writings of these early 'Fathers' of the Church. After all, unless one believes that the Church went seriously off the rails immediately after the death of the last apostle, this is how the apostolic teaching 'worked' in the life of ordinary congregations.

The men responsible for these writings (and they were all, so far as we can tell, *men*) were no plaster saints. Undoubtedly some of them had their own agendas, even scores to settle. And anyone suspected of heterodox views could expect short shrift. It is true that history tends to be written by the winners, so it is hard now to judge whether some of the 'alternative' movements in the early Church were quite as diabolical as they were painted. What cannot be doubted, I think, is the strength that the Church gained from unity, and the weakness it would have suffered if it had split into a hundred factions over various aspects of doctrine and practice. Clearly, these leaders had such issues in mind. Charity, one suspects, came a poor second to clarity.

But there *was* 'charity', in the sense that the apostle Paul defined it—*agape*, in Greek, self-giving love. Often the spirit of *agape* breathes through these writings. There was a deep and compelling love for the 'fellowship' and a willingness to give oneself not only for the 'cause' but for the 'others'. I doubt if any present-day Christian can read these writings without two emotions: pride (because these are our forerunners in the journey of faith) and humility (because we are not sure that under the same circumstances we would have the courage to act as they did).

What follows, then, are readings from the writings of the early Church—more or less, the first two centuries of the Christian era. They have been translated with some freedom, largely because it is often easier to convey the 'feel' as well as the meaning of Greek and Latin in paraphrase rather than strict word-for-word translation. Each author or source has a short introduction, which provides some background and context for the pieces.

This is definitely not a book for academic study of the Church Fathers. Rather, it's an attempt to bring something of the atmosphere, faith and life of those early years into the day-to-day experience of modern Christians. Their world is not, in many ways, our world, though many of the controversies which engaged so much of their attention are almost precisely the same as the ones that preoccupy us. They were not sure how to react to the prevailing culture, and divided between those who proposed outright opposition to every hint of pagan or 'philosophical' teaching and those who urged Christians to understand and relate their message to them. Some favoured a 'charismatic' approach; some sound remarkably like the seventeenth-century Puritans!

But if their arguments are ours, so is their Gospel, and their commission is ours, too—to make known the message of the risen

Lord Jesus to a people who are preoccupied with other things. In that, they were miraculously successful, turning the world upside down in the space of four or five generations. We simply *must* have something to learn from people who could do that.

Clement of Rome

Clement was one of the earliest Christian writers, born at about the time of the crucifixion of Jesus and so contemporary with many of the first Christians. He became known as the bishop (or overseer) of the church at Rome, which seems to have had from earliest times some role of seniority among the churches. At any rate, his letter appears to address trouble in the church at Corinth, which is quite a long way from Rome! It was written towards the end of the first century, which means that it is in the immediate post-apostolic era. Typically, Clement saw the issues facing the world at that time as a clash between darkness and light, good and evil, Satan and Christ. He was also sharply aware of the danger of divisions and splits in the Church and of the need for the Christians to hold fast to the faith in a culture that was highly suspicious of 'alien' cults and philosophies. The Church had already faced one period of vicious persecution which had possibly just ended with the assassination of the emperor Domitian in AD96, and its leaders feared that more, and possibly worse, lay ahead. For Clement, the answer was to hold fast—to the truth, to the Church and, above all, to Christ. His letter is steeped in the Old Testament Scriptures—sometimes various passages arbitrarily strung together, sometimes texts barely identifiable to the modern biblical scholar—but it also breathes a great atmosphere of Christian love and unity. He is familiar with some of the apostolic writings, notably of Paul and 1 Peter, and clearly 'breathes the same air' as they did.

1: Never too late

If we are ever tempted to feel that we have left repentance too late, or that we have persisted in sin for so long that we have exhausted God's patience, we should remember two things.

The first is that in every generation the Lord has offered the way of repentance to anyone who turns to him. It was true in the days of Noah, when those who took notice of his warnings and repented were saved. Long after, the people of Nineveh repented when Jonah preached to them about God's judgment. Although they were not his people, they turned to God in prayer and pleaded for forgiveness... and received it.

The constant message of our teachers, through the Holy Spirit, is repentance. 'By my oath,' the Lord himself declares, 'I do not want the sinner to die, but to repent.' And elsewhere in Scripture he says, 'Though your sins are as red as crimson, I will make them as white as snow.'

So it is God's own will that every one of his dear children should find that the door to repentance is always open. And when we enter it, we shall find how precious the blood of Christ is in God's eyes. For it is that blood, poured out for forgiveness, that offers grace to the whole of humankind.

CLEMENT OF ROME

2: God's patience

Think of a tree, when you are tempted to feel that God's promises are delayed, or when you begin to doubt that the Lord will come again, as he said he would. 'We have heard these promises in our fathers' time,' people say, 'and now we have grown old, and still these prophecies have not been fulfilled.'

Think of a tree, because the process of growth there is also slow, but yet inevitable. After harvest, the foliage falls. In winter the tree stands bare. But in the spring a bud appears, and from the bud come leaves, and later flowers. These in turn lead on to young, unripe grapes, and finally the full cluster of ripe fruit. It does not take very long, it's true, but the whole process must take place. No stage can be left out. There are no short cuts to a crop of good, mature fruit.

Neither can God's purposes be hurried. No stage can be left out. The whole process must take place. But let us be in no doubt that inevitably his purposes will be fulfilled. The Scripture says, 'He will surely come quickly, he will not delay... the Lord, the Holy One you wait for, will suddenly come to his temple.'

So, be ready!

CLEMENT OF ROME

⌘
3: Humility

My brothers and sisters, let's have some humility. Let's forget all this self-promoting and ego-boosting, and all this petty squabbling about status. Instead, let's start doing what the Bible commands. 'The wise man shouldn't boast of his wisdom, or the strong man of his strength, nor the rich man of his wealth. If we must boast, let's boast of what the Lord has done.'

Jesus had something to say about this, too. 'Be merciful,' he advised, 'and then people will have mercy on you. Forgive, and then others will forgive you. Treat others with kindness, and they will then treat you kindly. But if you constantly assume the role of critic, judging and condemning others, beware. One day the roles will change. You will stand before your judge, and he will condemn you.'

We should listen to these words and let them strengthen our determination to pursue true humility of mind. After all, it is God who says, 'Who wins my approval? The person who is gentle, calm… and trembles at my touch.'

CLEMENT OF ROME

4: A prayer in time of persecution

Teach us, Holy Father, to hope in your name,
You, from whom everything that exists has come into being.
Open our inward eyes to recognize you,
even though you are the highest in high heaven,
the Holy One among the ranks of all the holy.
You, Lord God, bring down the proud and outwit the cunning.
You promote the humble and make the arrogant fall.
You hold in your hand every issue of life:
whether we are to be poor or rich, whether we are to live or to die.
You see every spirit, good or evil, and read the inmost thoughts and
intentions of every heart.

When we are in danger, you come to our aid.
When we are feeling desperate, you save us from our sense of failure.
When events in the world overshadow us,
help us to remember who you are:
the Creator and Overseer of every living being.

CLEMENT OF ROME

5: A prayer for help

Through your work alone, Lord, you brought into being the eternal fabric of the creation. You created the earth. You are utterly faithful as the years roll by, absolutely just in your judgments, wonderful in majesty and power, infinitely wise and discreet in all that you do. You are full of grace to those who put their trust in you.

So, gracious and faithful Lord God, forgive each of us our sins, disobediences and failures. Don't add them up, but wash us clean with the pure water of truth, and 'guide our feet into the way of holiness, to do only that which is good and pleasing to you'.

Shelter us under your mighty hand, Lord, and by your powerful arm deliver us from all that is evil, including those who hate us without reason. Give peace and unity to us, and indeed to all the dwellers on the earth, as you gave to our fathers who called on you in holiness, faith and truth. And help us, for your sake, to be obedient not only to your great and glorious name, but (because they rule only by your will and power) to all those who rule and govern us on the earth.
CLEMENT OF ROME

6: Why we need each other

Friends, we are in a battle, so let's get on with it. But also let's remember who is in charge of operations.

We are all familiar with the way the Imperial Army operates in the field, each man giving instant and efficient obedience to his officer's orders. And this is true right through the army, from top to bottom, from the lowliest trooper to the highest general. Each man obeys the orders of the Emperor, which come to him through his immediate superior.

There is no other way to run an army. The Emperor himself cannot survive without the obedience of all those men who make up his military. But neither can they survive without the protection and guidance of the Emperor. The great cannot exist without the small, and the small cannot exist without the great.

This is true of every organism, including the Church of Christ. It is this mutual dependence, this fusion of different elements, which ensures the health and vigour of the whole organism. The body, for instance, needs both the head and the feet. The feet are useless without the head to tell them what to do and where to go, but the head is powerless to move the body without the 'obedience' and co-operation of the feet. Even our smallest and simplest organs are necessary and valuable. Every part works together in common obedience, if the body is to function properly. We need each other!

CLEMENT OF ROME

⌘

7: Trouble in the church

Suppose there is friction or bad feeling over something in your church. What should you do about it, especially if you are involved in the arguments and divisions yourself?

Not only that, but let's suppose that you are in the right, that the trouble is not your fault... and that you are a mature and compassionate person.

In that case, I suggest that you should say to the elders (lit: *presbyters*) and members of your church: 'If I am in any way the cause of this trouble, even unwittingly, or if my presence in any way serves to prolong or perpetuate it, I will move to another congregation, however inconvenient or humiliating an experience that might be. I will always go anywhere you wish, and do anything the congregation decides—anything, if it will contribute to peace among Christ's flock and its pastors.'

Anyone who adopts this attitude will deserve a high reputation among Christians, and God's approval. And he or she will be sure of a welcome by another congregation, for 'the earth is the Lord's, and everything in it'.

CLEMENT OF ROME

⌘

8: It is the humble who win

God's generosity is a wonderful thing, freely offered. But if we abuse it, turning on one another and destroying the fellowship of the church, that very generosity will be found to condemn us. After all, there is no greater sin than the sin against love.

The Spirit of the Lord is like a beam of light scanning the inner recesses of our being. Let's remember this. Not a single thought, not one twisted motive, escapes his notice. He probes everything, sees everything and is near us all the time.

So what sense is there in trying to run away from the will of God? Or, even worse, opposing him? Better by far to set ourselves to oppose his enemies, to reject their arrogance and to turn a deaf ear to their attempts to divide the church in their own special interests.

Let's realize that it is the truly humble spirit that always wins and the proud one that always loses in the end. God exalts the humble and humbles the proud. He is the one who examines our inmost thoughts and intentions. His is the breath that keeps us alive and he, in his own good time, will take it away. What can we do, any of us, but give him our reverence?

CLEMENT OF ROME

9: Enjoying our work

There's nothing wrong with work. After all, even the Lord and Architect of the universe not only 'worked' on his creation, but derived pleasure and satisfaction from it—he 'saw that it was good'. For his own delight he created the skies and set the stars in order, divided the dry land from the waters and marked out their boundaries. His work continued as he gave life to the animals that live on the land, as well as to the creatures that live in the waters. Finally, to complete his labours, he formed man from the dust of the ground, shaping him in his own likeness. Only then, his work ended, did he pause, satisfied, to rest and to give the creation his blessing.

So if God himself could find joy and satisfaction in his work— work well done, work completed—so may we. In fact, we already have his command to put all our energy and enthusiasm into our work, doing it 'heartily, as though for the Lord'. We already have his command—now we have added his example. Let's spare no effort to obey his will for us where our work is concerned.

CLEMENT OF ROME

10: Doing the work of God

There is never any need to feel ashamed of the money you earn, provided you do indeed earn it! But if you don't—if you're a half-hearted, unreliable employee—then, of course, you'll probably be embarrassed every time you meet your 'boss'.

For Christians, the 'boss' is God. That's why we should do our work with all our hearts and souls. We are answerable to him for the quality of our work—and it is simply impossible to avoid meeting the Lord! 'Look,' says Scripture, 'the Lord is approaching, bringing rewards, to pay each as his work deserves.'

So he tells us not to be lazy or inefficient in any piece of work we do. No one who does his or her work 'before the Lord' will miss their reward. Think of the angels, that vast company of heaven, spending every moment in his service, waiting instantly to obey each of his commands. 'Ten thousand times ten thousand stand before him and thousands upon thousands serve him, crying, "Holy, holy, holy, Lord God of hosts: all creation is full of his glory".'

That should be a picture for us of our work: our daily work, done for his glory; and our work of praise and witness in the Church, as we are gathered together in perfect unity to do his will.

CLEMENT OF ROME

11: The door to life

Loving one another and putting the welfare of others before our own—this is the open door to life: 'Open for me the gate of righteousness, that I may go in and praise the Lord; the righteous shall come in by it.' And this *is* the gate of righteousness and the gate of Christ, the door to life, the entrance into the place of blessing. That way is open only to those who pursue holiness and integrity, and avoid creating strife.

By all means master the great doctrines of the Christian faith, and defend them. By all means utter the secrets of God's revelation, evaluating and interpreting what you hear from the lips of others.

But the brighter your reputation in the church and the more

ordinary people look up to you, the harder it will be for you to be humble. It is at that moment, more than any other, that we should pray for the grace of humility and set our ambition firmly on serving and building up the people of God, rather than enriching our own reputations.

CLEMENT OF ROME

※

12: Sharing the gifts

Where our physical bodies are concerned, every part contributes something important to the whole. It is exactly the same with the Church, the body of Christ. Each of us should give way to our neighbour, recognizing the spiritual gifts that the Lord has given to them. So the strong should not overlook the problems of the weaker Christians, and the weak should recognize the gifts of those who are strong. Wealthy Christians should share their riches with the poorer members, and those who benefit from their generosity should thank God for it.

But it goes a little further than that. If one of you has a gift of 'wisdom', it should be expressed not just in words but also in action, in good deeds which are related to the needs of the whole 'body'. If someone else has the gift of modesty, then they should leave others to say how modest they are—to draw attention to it oneself is somewhat to contradict the claim! If another Christian has achieved self-control in sexual matters, it should not be a matter of boasting, but of recognizing this, too, as a gift from the Lord, not some self-achieved 'strength' of their own.

After all, we were nothing when we came into the world, and we owned nothing, either. Everything we have, physically, morally and spiritually, comes from him and is his gift. Glorify *him*!

CLEMENT OF ROME

13: Future joys

Some of God's marvellous gifts we can know already—the experience of a life lived free from the fear of death, the splendour of his sheer goodness, truth that is honest and complete, faith that gives assurance and confidence in God and a purity that is far better than self-indulgence. These gifts we know and enjoy already.

But there are other gifts of God which by their very nature we cannot possibly know yet. They can only be revealed at the appropriate time by the Creator and Father of eternity, and only he knows how magnificent they are. But if they are better than the gifts we know already, how wonderful, how utterly desirable they must be!

It is worth waiting patiently for such gifts. But it is also worth straining every nerve to achieve them, by fixing our minds on the Giver, by seeking to discover and then do his will for us and by renouncing deceit and pursuing truth. Most of all, we can achieve that goal by coming to Jesus Christ, our great high priest, who is our protector on earth and our appointed way to heaven. Through him alone our eyes can look up to the highest heaven—yes, even into the face of God. And through him the Father allows us to taste those wonderful future joys, the joys of eternity, all of which are 'in him'.
CLEMENT OF ROME

14: Peace and harmony

True, inward peace of mind: that must be our goal. After all, it was God's original plan for his children.

Look at him, our Father and Creator, and see in him all of those priceless and incomparable qualities of true peace. The eye of faith will note his inexhaustible patience, his infinite calms, and that in the whole vast complex of his creation there is not a single discordant note.

The skies revolve at his command, and do so in silent submission. Day silently gives way to night, night silently yields to day. The sun, moon and stars with infinite calm move without a sound along their appointed orbits. Vegetation silently springs out of the soil, to provide food for people and animals. Silently, in the depths of the sea, his law still rules; and silently it rules in the caverns and chasms of the earth.

And look at the harmony of what he has made—the intricate combination of seasons, winds and rains. The most minute being, the tiniest plant—each plays its part in the harmonious whole, a harmony planned by him for the good of the whole creation.

Those of us who have found our place in this perfect plan—a place of mercy in the Lord Jesus—should know better than anyone else how profound is that peace and how perfect that harmony.

CLEMENT OF ROME

⌘
15: Decently and in order

As God has revealed his wisdom to us and given us the privilege of searching the depths of his knowledge, we should be all the more ready to respond to it by obediently doing those things which he has commanded. Among them, he has called us to offer our service and sacrifice at the appointed hour and times, not in a careless or disorderly way. And he has himself chosen those people whom he wishes to perform these services, so that everything may be done decently and in the proper order. In the same way, under the old dispensation, the high priest had his allotted role, and so did the priests and Levites. And there were ordinances which were binding on all the people of God.

Under the new dispensation, the Messiah was sent by God, and he in turn sent the apostles, who received the gospel from the Lord Jesus Christ himself. So the apostles, knowing the divine authority for their calling (confirmed to them by his resurrection, by the word of God and by the Holy Spirit) went from district to district and from city to city preaching the message. From among their converts, chosen and tested by the Spirit, they appointed deacons and bishops to guide the Church of the future. So those who lead, and those who follow them, are blessed by God, for they follow the law and purpose of the Master.

CLEMENT OF ROME

⌘

16: The bond of love

Who can explain the bond of God's love? Who is able to tell its greatness and its beauty? Truly, words cannot describe the heights to which the love of God can lift us.

Love unites us to God. 'Love covers a multitude of sins.' Love bears all things, is patient and kind. There is nothing corrupt about love, and nothing proud. Love never sets out to divide or to undermine good order. Love does everything in a spirit of unity. In love God's chosen people are made perfect, and without love nothing is pleasing to God.

In love the Master welcomes us. For love, and love alone, by the will of the Father, Jesus shed his blood for us, giving his flesh for our flesh and his life for ours.

So let anyone who claims to know the love of Christ prove it by doing what he commands. That is the test of love: 'If you love me, keep my commandments.'

<small>CLEMENT OF ROME</small>

17: Giving and accepting correction

There will be those in our congregations who fall into sin. We should pray for them, that the gifts of meekness and humility may be theirs, so that they are willing to submit—not to us, of course, but to the will of God. If they do, then they will find that he is compassionate and forgiving, and will welcome them back into fellowship with him and the other believers.

But this is not simply a message for those who have fallen into sin. We all need correction from time to time, and the fellowship to which we belong is the right environment for it to be both given and received. This process of mutual 'correction', if done in a spirit of love, is absolutely good and enormously helpful, and we should never take it amiss or reject such correction out of hand. After all, it is a process which reunites us with the will of God. Doesn't the Scripture say, 'Do not reject the Lord's admonition, for if he inflicts pain he also then restores us.'

You see, my beloved, how wonderfully the Master protects those he corrects. He is like a good father, who only corrects us so that we may receive his mercy and forgiveness. That's what I call 'holy correction'.

<small>CLEMENT OF ROME</small>

18: A bishop's prayer

Grant, Lord, that we may have hope in you, the source of life itself and of the whole creation. Open our inward eyes to know you as the most high among the lofty ones and the most holy among the holy ones. While you humble the proud and bring the imaginings of rulers to nothing, you raise up the poor and exalt those who are weak. You, Lord, alone can look into the deepest recesses of darkness and the ingenuity of mankind, in order to help those in danger and rescue those in despair. You have chosen out from the multitudes of the nations a people for your own possession, those who love you through your Son Jesus Christ. Through him you have led us on the way, made us holy, and given us honour.

So we ask you, Master, to be our help and support—to save us when we go through times of anguish, to have mercy on us when we feel low, to raise to their feet those who have fallen on the way, to reveal your love to those in need of it, to heal the sick, to bring back to yourself those who have wandered from your fold, to feed the hungry, to release the prisoners, to lift up the weak and to strengthen the faint-hearted. Then 'all the nations will know that you alone are God', that Jesus Christ is your Son, and that we are your people.

CLEMENT OF ROME

Ignatius of Antioch

Ignatius was probably the third bishop of Antioch in the last decades of the first century, so he was a contemporary of Clement of Rome and would have overlapped the apostolic period. Indeed, tradition has it that he was 'taught by the apostles'—not an unlikely scenario, in view of his location at Antioch, one of the great scenes of apostolic activity in the early Church. Indeed, according to the book of Acts, the first Gentile church was planted at Antioch and it was there that the believers were first called 'Christians' (Acts 11:19–26).

In truth, not a great deal is known about Ignatius until his arrest, in one of the periodic Roman sweeps against dissident groups, among whom they included the Christians. With several others, he was ordered to be sent to Rome, there to be fed to the wild beasts in the arena. The journey there was a long one, under the supervision of ten armed guards, and during various 'stops' Ignatius took the opportunity to meet the leaders of local churches and to deliver to each of them a pastoral letter. It is these letters which form the substance of the heritage he has left to us.

During the course of the journey, Ignatius visited Laodicea, Philadelphia, Sardis and Smyrna, where representatives of the churches at Tralles, Magnesia and Ephesus had come to meet him and salute the martyr-designate. To each of these churches, and to the visiting leaders, he handed over a letter, and he also wrote a letter which was sent on ahead of him to the church at Rome, expressing his hope of meeting them in due course. The prisoners and escort then moved on to Troas, where Ignatius despatched three more letters, one to the church at Philadelphia, one to the congregation at Smyrna and a personal one to Polycarp, who was the bishop at Smyrna. In the course of history a number of pseudo-letters of Ignatius have appeared, but there is a general consensus among scholars that there are seven undoubtedly authentic ones. He was finally martyred in the Flavian amphitheatre in Rome on 19 December AD107, in the reign of the emperor Trajan.

Of all the writings from this period, these letters of Ignatius reveal the greatest warmth and humanity. Here was a man of serene and unquestioning faith, holy in the best sense of the word, deeply concerned for the well-being of his flock, wise and fearless. In a way that seems almost reckless, he embraced the thought of martyrdom—indeed, as the journey to Rome progressed he seemed to be longing for it to take place. He was held in enormous affection, almost veneration, by his contemporaries, as is demonstrated by the delegations of church leaders who came to meet him on his last journey.

The great themes of his letters are the need for unity in the Church, for sound teaching and for total (if necessary, sacrificial) commitment. Some have argued that his insistence on the authority of the bishops made him the prime mover towards a so-called 'monarchical' view of the episcopate. There can be no doubting his strong belief that the Church would fall apart if congregations began to undermine the authority and leadership of the bishops, but this must be seen in its context. Here was a Church without, as yet, a 'New Testament' or any accepted credal statements to provide doctrinal order and stability. It was 'founded upon the apostles and prophets, Jesus Christ himself being the chief corner stone' (Ephesians 2:20).

But now that the apostles were probably all dead, where was the source of authority in the Church? For Ignatius, there was only one answer—in those 'bishops' (and he often included with them the 'presbyters' or elders, and deacons) who had been appointed to exercise apostolic leadership and order in the Church. But there is no suggestion in his writings that he wished to 'magnify' the role of the bishop. For him, it was simply a matter of practicality. How, apart from obedience to 'the bishop and his ministers', would the unity of the Church be maintained? For him, the only alternative would be sectarianism or a selfish kind of congregationalism—both of them anathema to him, because they undermined the great vision of the holy, catholic, apostolic Church which he believed had been handed on to them by the apostles themselves. The seeds of heresy were already sprouting, with Docetism (which taught that Christ had only the 'appearance' (*dokesis* in Greek) of a human being, and a resurgent Judaism (of the kind Paul denounced in Galatians), which once again threatened the great gospel doctrines of grace and faith.

But it is in his death that Ignatius is chiefly remembered, and especially in his vision of martyrdom as the ultimate proof of discipleship. It was for this that Ignatius was revered throughout the early Church. Martyrdom may not have much appeal for Christians in the Western world of today, but modern times, too, have seen their martyrs, notably in Africa and China. There, and elsewhere, the old saying has proven true: 'The blood of the martyrs is the seed of the Church'. Ignatius of Antioch would agree with that!

19: Working together

In the process of learning—which is what Christian discipleship really is—we all need to work together. Sometimes we shall wrestle together with some problem; sometimes we shall face together a common objective. We all share the same kinds of anxieties and disappointments; we all share the same moments of tranquillity as we rest in the Lord, and the same moments when we are called to rise together to some new challenge. We are all members of God's household—his stewards, his assistants, his servants.

Or, to change the metaphor, we are all soldiers in his army, in the pay of a commander whom we are called to satisfy by our service. Let there be no deserters from his ranks! Regard your baptism into Christ as a shield and your faith in him as a helmet for protection, and your patient endurance as armour around your body. Your weapon of attack is nothing but love.

You know how soldiers often put their pay into a savings account, so that one day they can draw out what they have earned. Let us learn from them, and lay up a deposit of good actions, of kind deeds, which on 'that day' we shall be able to draw upon in heaven.
IGNATIUS OF ANTIOCH

20: The two images

Everything has to come to an end one day, including human life, and that leaves us with two alternatives to consider. I shall call them 'life' and 'death'. Just as certainly, each of us will have to go to our appointed destination.

Look at it this way. There are two coinages in circulation. One is the currency of God's kingdom and the other is the currency of the world. The coins bear the stamp, the image, of the one who minted them. Christians bear the stamp and image of God the Father, imprinted on them by Jesus Christ. Unbelievers carry the print and image of the world. Only those who have shared in the death of the Lord Jesus truly bear his image and share in his risen life. The alternative is death. That is the choice.

Now, since I have seen you all with the eyes of faith, and embraced your whole congregation through the delegation who came to meet me, let me urge you to unity and godly love. Accept the bishop's authority as from God, and his ministers as the voice of the apostles. Entrust my particular friends, your deacons, with the responsibility of leading you in Christian service and worship. They are servants of Jesus Christ, the one who shared God's nature from all eternity and who has been revealed on earth in these recent times.

Be considerate to one another. Love each other consistently, after the example of Jesus Christ himself. And allow nothing of any kind to exist among you which could cause division, or weaken your unity with your bishop and leaders.

IGNATIUS OF ANTIOCH

✿

21: Salted with Christ

Imagine what it would be like if the Lord treated us in the way we treat others! It would be unbearable. We take his goodness for granted, whereas in fact we should learn from it how to live as Christians.

Our lives should be bursting with enthusiasm. Unfortunately, only too often we look like bread made with stale yeast—heavy and stodgy. It is Jesus himself who is the 'yeast' in our lives, lifting our spirits and infusing us with fresh lightness and flavour.

Or consider another illustration. You can tell if meat is good by its smell. If it's been properly salted and cured, it smells good. If it's been inadequately salted, or the salt has lost its properties, then it smells terrible! We are to be salted with Christ, so that we smell sweet and attractive to those around us. If we are not salted by him, then we shall have the smell of spiritual decay about us. Shallow faith and shallow attitudes undermine the work of Christ in us.

So, hold unshakeably to the heart of our faith, which is Jesus Christ our hope—born, crucified and risen, during the time when Pontius Pilate was governor. Let nothing turn you aside from that hope.

IGNATIUS OF ANTIOCH

—————————— ⌘ ——————————

22: When to be silent

There are two qualities that define the Christian life—faith, which is its beginning, and love, which is its goal. And they are attributes of God himself. All that makes for holiness flows from them, for no one who truly believes in God will commit sin, and no one who wholly loves can feel hatred.

We recognize a tree by its fruit and we ought to be able to recognize Christians by their actions. The fruit of faith should be evident in our lives, for being a Christian is much more than simply professing certain beliefs. True faith should reveal itself in practical and visible ways.

Indeed, it is much better to keep quiet about our beliefs but live them out, than to talk eloquently about what we believe and then contradict it by the way we live. Of course, it is very commendable to share the Christian faith with others, but only if the instructor is practising what he preaches!

After all, the great Teacher, Jesus, whose words carried

miraculous powers, also spoke eloquently by his silences. It's very revealing to notice how often Jesus said nothing, but by his actions or his attitude, or simply by the force of his personality, achieved the perfect result. That is a mark of spiritual maturity—to know when to speak, and when to be silent.

IGNATIUS OF ANTIOCH

⌘

23: Don't fall back

If we are still hankering after the rules and regulations of Judaism, it shows that we have failed to receive the grace of Jesus Christ. After all, he is the very one whose coming was foretold by the great Jewish prophets, who were inspired by the promise of God's Messiah.

You can look around at the church today and see in it people who formerly followed the Jewish religion but have now embraced this new hope. They believe, as we do, that God revealed himself in Jesus Christ, his very Word uttered out of the silence of eternity. They, like us, have been freed from slavery to rules and regulations. Indeed, they have even given up keeping the Sabbath, preferring instead to recognize the Lord's Day, the day when life broke through in the resurrection of Jesus, who died for us. It is his death which is the very heart of the mystery of the faith we hold and in which we are saved—whatever our detractors may say!

So how can Christians be drawn back into a religion that ignores the fact that Christ, the Messiah, has come? How can we live as though he had never been born, or died, or risen from the dead? The prophets of Israel looked eagerly forward to what we have been privileged to experience—that's why the risen Jesus visited them in the place of death and raised them to life [see 1 Peter 3:19–20]. No one should take this great privilege lightly.

IGNATIUS OF ANTIOCH

24: Our attitude to 'unbelievers'

What should be our attitude to those around us who are not Christians? Certainly we should pray for them, not just occasionally or as a matter of duty, but all the time, in the hope that they will have a change of heart and so find their way to God.

But we should also give them every opportunity to learn the truth of Christ from us, not so much, perhaps, by our preaching to them in so many words, but by the way we behave towards them. Our attitude should reflect the attitude of Christ.

So, when they are hostile, meet them with gentleness. When they angrily accuse us of something, respond with calm words. When they abuse us, pray for them. It is possible to stand firm against violence and error while remaining perfectly calm and gentle. Don't be drawn into playing their game! At the same time, don't let us compromise our beliefs or water them down to make them more acceptable.

Let's show them that we regard them as children of the one Creator, and simply want them to become also sons and daughters of the same Father, our brothers and sisters in Christ. As I have said, our attitude should be that of the Lord Jesus. If we imitate him, we won't go wrong.

IGNATIUS OF ANTIOCH

25: The death of superstition

I am now the servant of the Cross—the Cross which appals and repels the unbeliever, but which means life and health to us. 'Where is your wise man now and where is your clever debater?' Where are the sophisticated words of our 'intellectuals'? God has acted. Jesus Christ has come, conceived of Mary of David's ancestry and of the Holy Spirit, born, baptized, suffering and triumphant.

Until these days, evil forces have dominated the world—magic, evil spirits, superstition. But the coming of Jesus took them by surprise. Even the 'prince of this world' was totally unaware of what was happening in Mary's womb. He did not realise the deep significance of the birth of Jesus, nor of his crucifixion. God hoodwinked the powers of evil, outwitted them and defeated them by his own, silent wisdom, by three mysterious cries from the heart of the universe—birth, death, resurrection.

How was the secret of the coming of Jesus announced to the world? Why, a star shone, more brilliant than the rest. It baffled the 'experts', the seers, the men of magic. They had no explanation for its sudden appearance.

But with that star a new age dawned, for the old powers of magic and sorcery were broken and superstition received its death-blow. The age-old empire of evil superstition crumbled, because God was now appearing in human form to bring in his new age, a new kingdom and a new life that never ends.

IGNATIUS OF ANTIOCH

⌘
26: No illusion

If you come across anybody who says that Jesus Christ never lived, or that he's just an 'idea' or a myth—shut your ears to him! Jesus was born into a human family, a descendant of David. His mother was Mary. He was persecuted and crucified under Pontius Pilate. These are facts testified to us by some who are now in heaven, and by some who are still alive on earth. We have met these people!

How can Jesus be a phantom? How can his life be an illusion or a myth? These are facts of history.

It is also a fact that he rose from the dead, or rather, that his Father raised him up. And that is the most important 'fact' of all, because Jesus promised that the Father would also raise us up, if we believe in him. So if Christ Jesus is *not* alive, neither shall we be. There is nothing left for us to hope for if he is merely an idea or a fantasy.

In any case, if he only *appeared* to live, and only *appeared* to die, and only *appeared* to rise from the dead—why should I be prepared to be put in chains for such a 'myth'? Why should I be ready to die for an 'illusion'? I am prepared to die for him, the true and real Son of God. But no one is prepared to die for a shadow!

IGNATIUS OF ANTIOCH

⌘

27: Upward to the light

All the way from Syria to Rome I have been chained to a detachment of soldiers who have behaved like animals towards me. I tried giving them money, but the more I gave them the more roughly they treated me. Quite honestly, they are like a pack of leopards, enjoying their role as hunters, with me as the prey.

Well, that has some advantages. I may as well get used to 'leopards' now. It will be lions, and real ones at that, when I get to Rome. So I can make some progress towards preparing myself spiritually and mentally for what lies ahead.

All I pray is that, when the moment comes, the lions will be quick about it. Some Christians have suffered torments because the animals have toyed with them. If my lions are like that, I shall antagonize them!

Forgive me for writing like this, but I do know what is best for me. No power, human or spiritual, must hinder my coming to Jesus

Christ. So whether the way is to be fire, or crucifixion, or wild beasts in the arena, or the mangling of my whole body, I can bear it provided I am assured that it is the way to him.

And it is. All the riches and power in the world cannot compare with that. So far as I am concerned, to die in Jesus Christ is better than to be king of the whole wide world! Do not try to tempt me to stay here by offering me the world and its attractions. Just let me make my way upward to that pure and undiluted light.

IGNATIUS OF ANTIOCH

✧

28: The power of prophecy

Now of course I am not infallible! Like everyone else, I can be mistaken. But the Holy Spirit can't be mistaken, nor can he be deceived, because he is the Spirit of God, and God is infallible.

Let me give you an example. When I visited the church at Philadelphia there was a faction there, a group who were undermining the church's leadership and constantly opposing their decisions. Now God is my witness that I knew nothing about this at all. No one had told me of it and no rumour of it had reached my ears.

So when I stood up to prophesy, and shouted in a loud voice, 'Give more respect to your bishop, your elders and your deacons!' it was the Holy Spirit who was speaking in me. Although I know some people think I had been told in advance of the divisions at Philadelphia, and spoke from prior knowledge, the absolute truth is that this was the voice of God alone.

So, remember that, and remember and obey the other things I said as well: 'Keep your bodies as temples of God. Love unity. Shun divisions. Follow Jesus Christ, as he followed his Father.'

IGNATIUS OF ANTIOCH

29: A martyr's prayer

All the corners of the earth and all the kingdoms of the world have no appeal to me. So far as I am concerned, it is better to die for Jesus Christ, united to him, than to be monarch of earth's greatest kingdom. All I seek is the one who died for me; my only desire is to know his risen life. It's as though I am going through labour in childbirth. Don't shut me out from the experience of life—don't condemn me to being stillborn. Here is a man whose only longing is to belong to God. Don't try to persuade him to sell out to the world's values, or to entrance him with its delights. Leave me to follow the path of suffering taken by my Lord. If you have any understanding of God's life in you, you will appreciate how I feel and the driving force that impels me towards the goal.

The prince of this world would like to get at me and undermine my resolve. Please don't help him! Instead, back me up in my purpose, because I am sure it is God's purpose, too. Don't have Jesus on your lips but the world in your hearts, thinking of ways of dissuading me from my course—not even were I to come and beg you to do it. Take this written instruction as my unshakeable and true intention. Honestly, and writing as someone fully and satisfyingly alive at this moment, I am longing for the death that lies ahead of me, longing with the passion of a lover. All I can hear, above the voices of the world, is a breath of life within me that whispers, 'Come to the Father!'
IGNATIUS OF ANTIOCH

The Teacher (*Didache*)

First seeing the light of day in 1883, ten years after its discovery in the library of a Constantinople monastery, the *Didache*, as it became known, is undoubtedly one of the oldest Christian manuscripts which we possess. It was found with other ancient documents, including the Letters of Ignatius and Clement and the 'Epistle of Barnabas', but it is different in style and purpose from these more personal writings. The *Didache* (the word simply means 'Teaching') was quite clearly intended as a manual of instruction for the early Church, possibly for use with those being prepared for baptism. Its anonymous author or compiler (for it seems to have more than one source) drew on existing teaching from Judaism, giving it a Christian application where appropriate, but also set out detailed instructions about the conduct of baptisms and the eucharist. For these reasons, it is a uniquely valuable insight into the life of the Church in the immediate post-apostolic period, until a clear structure began to emerge in the middle of the second century.

The *Didache* sets out in graphic style the two ways of life open to people: the Way of Death and the Way of Life. This is reminiscent of Christ's teaching about the 'broad and narrow ways' (Matthew 7:13–14). The Teacher also has a powerful passage on the second coming and the final judgment, issues which were to feature prominently in the life of the early Church.

There is some dispute about the date of authorship or compilation of the *Didache*, but it was certainly completed before AD150.

30: The two paths

The Way of Life is this: love the Lord your God who made you, and your neighbour as you love yourself. And do not do to others what you would not want them to do to you.

Give to anyone who asks you, without seeking repayment or reward, because the Father loves us to share his generosity with others. Those who give in this way will be blessed by God—there is no fault in such actions. But the one who receives such a gift should beware, because although there is no blame attached to accepting a gift which we actually need, it is wrong to accept it if we are not in need. Indeed, the one who does so may be held to account for his behaviour. There is good sense in the old saying, 'Let your alms grow damp with the sweat of your palm, until you know who it is you are giving to.'

To avoid the Way of Death, steer clear of evil people. Don't give way to anger, which can lead to violence. Equally, abstain from any form of fanaticism, quarrelling and strife. The younger men, especially, must beware of sexual sin, including impure talk and a 'roving eye'—these can be the first steps on the road to adultery or fornication.

Have nothing to do with omens, astrology or magic—in fact, don't even agree to be present when such things occur, because they can lead to the sin of idolatry. Avoid lies, for lying leads to other dishonesty. Don't be ambitious for riches or public praise— another pitfall for the unwary. And don't grumble, or push your opinions on others, or allow yourself to dwell on what is evil. Learn to be meek, for the meek will have the earth for their possession. Be patient with others, kind, open-hearted, calm and good. And never forget the teaching you have received.

THE *DIDACHE*

31: The Way of Life

This is the Way of Life. Accept as good every experience of life that comes your way, in the belief that nothing can happen to you outside the will of God.

Night and day, respect those who speak the word of God to you, because wherever the attributes of the Lord are spoken of, he is present. So honour those who preach about him. Spend as much time as you can in the company of your fellow Christians, because their way of life will support yours. Don't take sides in disputes in the church, but try to encourage peace between those who disagree. Try to judge situations fairly. If necessary, correct people without fear or favour, and once you have come to a decision, stick to it.

When it comes to Christian giving, don't be like those who are always ready to take (when they get the chance) but manage to be absent when the time comes for giving! If you have done well, regard your offering as some small expression of gratitude for the forgiveness of your past sins. Give without holding back and without grudging, and you will see how generously the great Giver will reward you. Don't turn your back on those in need. Indeed, be ready to share your possessions with your fellow Christian, not claiming a right to anything as your own. After all, you are joint inheritors of a heavenly kingdom, so why not share the rewards of the earthly one, too?

If you have servants who are Christians, trusting in the same Lord as you do, speak to them politely, even when giving them orders. If you are rude to them, they may cease to honour the One who is over you both. He doesn't call us according to our social standing, but according to the working of his Spirit. Those of you who are servants should treat your Christian employers with proper respect and honour, as representatives of God's authority.

Don't neglect these commandments of the Lord, keeping them without any additions or alterations. Confess your faults in church, and make sure that when you turn to prayer it is with a cleansed conscience.

This is the Way of Life.

THE *DIDACHE*

⌘

32: Rules for worship

On the Lord's Day, come together to break bread and offer the eucharist. Before you do, be sure to make full confession of your sins, so that your offering of worship may be undefiled. Anyone who has a disagreement with a fellow Christian is not to take part until they have been reconciled. For the Lord has said, 'Everywhere and always bring me a sacrifice that is undefiled, for I am a great king, says the Lord, and my Name is the wonder of the nations.'

Choose as your leaders—bishops and deacons—those who are worthy of the Lord's approval: humble, not eager for money, but sincere and genuine. After all, with the apostles* (evangelists) and prophets, they should be honoured as your teachers and leaders. If you have to reprove one another, do it peaceably and not in the heat of the moment, as the Gospel tells us. Have nothing to do with a Christian who has hurt his neighbour—at least, not until he repents.

In short, in your prayers, your Christian giving and in all your activities, make the Gospel of the Lord Jesus Christ your only guide.

THE *DIDACHE*

---

* 'Apostles' here are not the Twelve, of course, but those who fulfilled, like them, an itinerant ministry of church-planting.

33: The last days

Guard your way of life. Don't let your lamps go out or be caught unprepared. Be ready, because you simply do not know the moment when the Lord will return.

Come together often, to strengthen each other spiritually, because all your past faithfulness will be no help at that moment, if you have not remained constant in your faith. For in those last days false prophets and deceivers will be everywhere, trying to lead the flock astray. Some 'sheep' will turn into 'wolves', and love will turn to hate, betrayal and persecution.

At that point the great Deceiver will appear, pretending to be the Son of God and performing miracles and wonders. The whole world will fall into his hands and evil will dominate as it has never done before. All the human race will be put on trial, as it were—a trial by fire. Many will fail the test and perish. But those who hold fast to the faith will be saved by the One who bore the curse of sin on our behalf.

Then the signs of truth will appear: the skies will open, the trumpet will sound, the dead will be raised. And then the Lord will come, bringing all his holy ones with him. And every eye shall see him riding on the clouds of heaven.

THE *DIDACHE*

34: Welcoming true prophets

You should welcome to your church every prophet who truly comes 'in the Name of the Lord', though that doesn't mean that you may not need to apply certain sensible tests. In this way, you will sort out the genuine from the false prophet. If he is passing through on his way to somewhere else, you should give him all the help you can, but he shouldn't stay more than two or three days with you, unless it is unavoidable. Of course, if he wants to settle down in your town and has some suitable skills, then encourage him to find a job to earn a living. If he has no trade or skills, you will need to have the wisdom to discern whether he is genuine, or just trying to sponge off you on the strength of being a fellow Christian. You must be on your guard against those who are, to put it bluntly, trying to exploit Christ.

A genuine prophet, however, who wants to settle down and make his home among you, has every right to a livelihood. In the same way, a genuine teacher should be paid for his ministry, just as you would pay a manual worker for his toil. Indeed, you should take tithes of the winepress and the grain harvest, giving them to the prophets (or, if you have no prophets, to the poor). That's the equivalent of the priestly tithes in former times. So when you bake a batch of loaves, or open a new cask of wine, remember to give the first tenth to those who have need, whether because of their ministry in your church or through poverty. In that way, you will be keeping God's commandment.

THE DIDACHE

The Epistle of Barnabas

In about AD 130, a piece of Christian writing came on to the scene which was to achieve considerable repute in the early Church. It was known as 'The Epistle of Barnabas', and indeed was thought by some, though not all, of the early Fathers to have been written by Paul's colleague and fellow missionary (see Acts 13—15). In fact, this is virtually impossible, both from internal evidence and from the probable date of authorship. The author may have been named 'Barnabas', of course, but his approach was far from the gentle and encouraging style of the apostle's companion. He is, in fact, a polemicist against the Jewish religion, which may well have been undergoing something of a resurgence under the more benevolent reign of the emperor Hadrian. For Barnabas, the Jewish religion is intrinsically wrong, even evil. All of its greatest truths, ceremonies and laws were nothing but 'types' (allegorical symbols) of truths ultimately fulfilled in Christ, and much of his Epistle is taken up with a meticulous—but often to the modern reader quite fanciful —allegorizing of Old Testament stories, events and ceremonies.

However, the work is important to the modern reader of the Bible for several reasons. The first is that Barnabas shows the extent and passion of the division between Judaism and Christianity during this period of history. This was partly because most of the first Christians were converts from Judaism—almost certainly Barnabas himself was—and there is no protagonist quite so fierce as a convert from one cause to another. It was also the result of the Church moving increasingly, and successfully, into the Greco-Roman world, with its altogether different culture and approach to religion. And thirdly it was because all through the early days of the Church there was a quite strident party of 'Judaizers', who were intent on ensuring that Christianity remained what it had at first seemed to be, a particular sect within Judaism. For these people, the food laws and Jewish festivals were crucial tests for new disciples. We can see these disputes emerging in the apostolic period (Acts 15:1; Galatians 2:11–13), and they had obviously not gone away nearly a century later.

Eventually the Church and Judaism went their separate ways, though not without rancour, which may help to account for, though not excuse, the rabid anti-semitism of some early Christian writings.

However, the value of the Epistle of Barnabas to the modern reader is not solely as an example of second-century polemics! The author's allegorical method of interpreting Scripture was highly regarded in the first centuries of the Christian era, and, in some sections of the Church, has persisted to the present day. In this approach (which we can also find in the Epistle to the Hebrews, for example) the value of the Hebrew Scriptures lies mainly in the way they provide models and antetypes of Jesus Christ. Indeed, every detail of such passages as the description of the building of the tabernacle could be given allegorical significance, even down to curtains, ewers and hinges on doors. One early Father, applying the same technique to the Gospels, saw the two coins given by the good Samaritan to the innkeeper in advance payment for the traveller's convalescence as 'types' of the two sacraments (baptism and the eucharist). It is a preaching style some of us can remember from younger days and it is probably still practised today. At any rate, it is an element in scriptural interpretation which the modern reader cannot afford to ignore—and, of course, in some instances it is entirely valid and consistent with the way Jesus himself applied the Old Testament prophecies and stories to his own ministry (see, for instance, Matthew 12:39–41 and 16:4).

Barnabas has a cavalier attitude to citations from the Old Testament, generally using the Septuagint (Greek) version of the text but interpreting it liberally to suit his own arguments. He carries this so far at times that it is difficult to establish which passage of Scripture he had in mind. Whatever else they were, these early Christian preachers were not 'fundamentalists', in the modern sense!

In the following extracts from the Epistle of Barnabas we shall concentrate on passages where the writer uses this approach to the Hebrew Scriptures to illuminate the incarnation and passion of Christ. Here we can see how powerful a tool the Old Testament can be in the hands of a skilful preacher—especially, of course, one who did not have a New Testament at all.

35: Looking at the Son

We know that the Lord was willing to undergo suffering in his deep concern for our salvation. Nevertheless, he is Lord of all the earth, to whom God at the very beginning spoke these words: 'Let us make man in our own image and likeness.' If that is so, how could he put himself in the position of suffering at the hands of mortal men? Listen, and I will tell you.

The divinely inspired prophets had foretold his coming long before, and since it was essential for him to appear in human flesh if he were to destroy death and reveal that the dead can rise again, he voluntarily chose to become man and to suffer for us. By so doing, he could fulfil the divine promises made to our ancestors, and establish a new people for his own possession. He could also demonstrate, through his presence on earth, that it was God's intention to raise mankind from the dead, and after that to judge them. More than that, by the teaching which he gave to the people of Israel and by his signs and wonders, he revealed the infinite depth of his mercy. That is shown in his choice of the apostles, the men who were charged to preach the good news. Some of these men were no better than villains of the worst sort, which proves that Jesus came 'not to call saints, but sinners'.

Furthermore, if he had not come in the flesh, how could human beings have ever 'looked on him and been saved', as the invitation of the Prophet suggests? For when we look at the brightness of the sun we are blinded by it, even though it is itself God's handiwork and will one day cease to exist. We cannot look directly at God in his glory, but we can look at the Son of God, come in our flesh, and see God's glory in him.

EPISTLE OF BARNABAS

36: The land of milk and honey

Moses said to the people of Israel, 'Look, this is what the Lord God says: Enter into the good land which the Lord vowed he would give to Abraham and Isaac and Jacob. Take it as your inheritance. It is a land flowing with milk and honey.'

Now let me show you what true understanding can tell us about that passage. What it is, in fact, saying is this: 'Put your trust in Joshua—the Joshua who will come to you in human form.' ['Joshua' and 'Jesus' are the same word in Hebrew.] What is this 'land', then? Why, it is humankind, because we were created out of the very earth itself—remember how God made Adam from the dust of the ground? And what is this 'good land' promised to us— the one 'flowing with milk and honey'? The prophet is speaking here in a divinely inspired allegory, which requires a wise and instructed mind to interpret it. You see, when the Lord gave us new birth as new people through the forgiveness of our sins by the work of Joshua/Jesus, he made us into a completely new race, an entirely new creation. So the 'new land' is the 'new humankind', ourselves —the ones he has brought into the place flowing with milk and honey.

But what is the 'milk and honey'? Well, a baby starts its life by drinking only milk, and then, when it has grown a little, moves on to honey. In the same way, when we have begun the new life of faith we are fed with the milk of the Word, but the promise is that we shall go on, like the Israelites of old entering Canaan, to 'rule the land'—to exercise God's authority over the earth itself. Then we, the children of joy, will taste the honey of his promises!

EPISTLE OF BARNABAS

37: The people of the Covenant

Who are the people of the New Covenant? We are—it belongs to us. Let us see how that came about. The truth is, the Lord himself gave us this privilege, making us the people of his inheritance through suffering on our behalf. It is true that the incarnation of Jesus gave the people of the Old Covenant their opportunity to enter into the new one, but they rejected it. That is how we have been able to receive the inheritance of the Lord Jesus from its rightful heir, the one to whom God himself had granted it. This was why he was sent into the world—to reveal the divine love in his own humanity, to free our hearts from the mists of darkness and death (to which our evil had long abandoned us) and to establish this new Covenant with us through his Word.

After all, the Bible itself tells us that this was the Father's purpose in sending his Son into the world—to ransom us from darkness and transform us into a holy people for himself. 'I have appointed you,' God says through the prophet Isaiah, 'to make a covenant with the people and to be a light to the nations; to open the eyes of the blind, to free the captives from their chains and those who are in darkness from the prison-house.' This is how we know the depths from which we have been saved, but it is also how we know the 'good news of grace to the lowly'.

EPISTLE OF BARNABAS

38: The true Temple

We come now to the subject of the Temple—and I want to emphasize how foolish it was of people ever to pin their hopes on a mere building, as if that could be the dwelling-place of God himself, their Creator. What does the Lord himself say about this? Listen to these words from the prophet Isaiah: 'Heaven is my throne, and the earth my footstool. So how can you build a house for me, and what would it be like, and where is the place on earth that could serve as my resting-place?' You can see from this that to pin one's hopes on a man-made temple is sheer folly.

But Isaiah also prophesies that the very people who pulled the Temple down will one day rebuild it (49:17*). And that promise is in the process of being fulfilled now. Yes, the Temple and the city in which it stood have been demolished, as God had foretold, but it is being rebuilt.

You see, the destruction of the man-made Temple did not mean that there can be no temple of God at all. Of course there can! The prophet Daniel tells us that 'when the week draws to a close a glorious temple of God will be built in his Name' [possibly a reference to 9:24]. So there *will* be a temple, a new one, built 'in the Name of the Lord'.

It comes about in this way. In the days before we believed in the Lord, our hearts were a rotten and insecure foundation for any spiritual building. Indeed, by our opposition to the will of God we had made ourselves into nothing less than a chamber of idolatry, a dwelling-place for all that is evil. Then we were 'a temple made with hands'.

But when through Jesus, and through putting our trust in him, we experienced forgiveness of our sins, we were made new, truly a

* In the Greek (Septuagint) version used in the early Church.

'new creation' at the hands of God. As a result of that transformation, the Lord himself now actually dwells in these miserable habitations! Yes, *he lives in us*. We are his new Temple, the place where he dwells.

And if we ask how this can be, the answer lies in the saving message of the faith, in his gracious calling, and in the wisdom of his teaching and precepts. It lies in the truth of his very presence inwardly inspiring us. It lies in the way he has opened our reluctant lips (like the closed gates of the Temple!) to confess him and in his gift of true repentance. It is in these ways, my children, that he has admitted us, who are really the slaves of mortality, into the true Temple of God, the dwelling-place of immortality.

EPISTLE OF BARNABAS

Polycarp of Smyrna

Polycarp of Smyrna, who ranks alongside Ignatius of Antioch as a pillar of the Church in the days immediately after the apostles, was probably born in AD69. His pupil, Irenaeus, tells us that as a boy Polycarp was 'taught by the apostles and met many people who had seen Christ'. The fact that he lived until AD155, when he was martyred, means that he is a major link between the world of the apostolic Church and the emerging Church of the following centuries. One thing is certain: he was greatly distressed by the growth of what he saw as 'false teaching', and dedicated his own ministry to the faithful and meticulous transmission of the truths he had been taught in earlier days.

Early records suggest that he met the apostle John and sat at his feet. Some even claim that it was John who appointed Polycarp to be bishop of Smyrna, on the coast of Asia Minor not far from Ephesus. He remained as bishop for fifty years, until his arrest, with a number of other Christians in the city, during a time of persecution. Now an old man in his eighties, he was taken to the public arena, where he met his fate with courage and dignity. The church at Smyrna later circulated an account of his martyrdom, which became one of the jewels of early Christian literature.

It seems appropriate, then, to begin this short section of readings from his writings with an extract from this account—the earliest genuine record of a Christian martyrdom after the period of the Acts of the Apostles.

39: The martyrdom of Polycarp

After his arrest, his captors put him on an ass and led him into the city. It was a Greater Sabbath, and the Commissioner of Police, Herod, and his father Nicetas, came out to meet him. They tried to persuade him that there could be no harm in simply saying, 'Caesar is Lord' and offering a little incense at his shrine. That way, he could save his life. At first, the bishop was silent, but as they persisted he said, 'No, I reject such advice.' Having failed with persuasion, they then tried threatening him, manhandling him roughly out of the carriage so that his shins were rapped. But he walked briskly with them, not even looking back, as they led him towards the arena, where there was such an uproar going on that no one could make himself heard.

As Polycarp entered the arena, a voice was heard from heaven: 'Be strong, Polycarp, and hold fast.' No one saw the one who spoke, but Christians who were present certainly heard it. Finally, the bishop was brought forward for formal examination, and at this point, as people recognized who it was, a deafening clamour broke out. The Governor then asked him to identify himself, and tried to persuade him to recant his beliefs. 'Act with the dignity of your advanced years,' he advised. 'Swear an oath in the name of Caesar, admit you have been in error and denounce those infidels who defy the Emperor.'

At that point, Polycarp turned his gaze on the crowd in the stands and then, indicating their ranks with a sweep of his hand, and looking up to heaven, he cried. 'Down with the infidels!'

Still the Governor went on trying to persuade him. 'Take the oath, and I will release you. Renounce your Christ.'

Polycarp replied with these words. 'Eighty-six years I have served him, and he has never done me any wrong. How can I then blaspheme my King and my Saviour?'

Still the Governor persisted. 'Swear in the name of Caesar.' But the bishop answered, 'How can you think that I would swear in the name of Caesar, as though I did not know who I am? Let me tell you plainly that I am a Christian, and if you would like to know what that means, let us fix a time and give me a hearing.' The Governor suggested he might try his arguments on the screaming crowd instead, but Polycarp said, 'I had hoped that you, to whom I have been taught to pay proper respect as one appointed by God to civil power and authority, might wish to consider such things rationally. It would be a waste of time trying to persuade this crowd.'

At this point the Governor resorted to threats. 'I have wild beasts here. If you don't recant, I shall have you thrown to them.' 'Call them up,' replied Polycarp, 'for it is out of the question for me to exchange the right way of thinking for the wrong one. On the other hand, it would be very creditable for you to change over from the wrong to the right.'

The Governor put it to him directly: 'If you do not recant, I will have you burnt to death, since you seem to think so lightly of being fed to the animals.'

'The fire you threaten me with,' replied the old man, 'cannot go on burning for ever; eventually it will go out. But the flames of God's judgment, of which you seem to be completely unaware, are kept for those who reject him, and they burn for ever. Why do we go on wasting time? Bring out whatever you wish.' As he spoke these words, he was filled with courage and joy and his whole face shone with grace. The Governor now seemed to be completely at a loss. In fact, what he did was to send a crier into the arena to announce three times, 'Polycarp has admitted to being a Christian!' At these words the whole audience, both the heathen and the Jews who were there, broke into screams of uncontrollable anger... and there were demands that a lion should be released to attack him. When they were told that this was no longer possible, the Governor having ruled it out, they cried for him to be burnt alive.

In no time a massive fire was kindled. When it was ready,

Polycarp stripped off his outer garments and his girdle, and even tried to remove his shoes, which he had always carefully kept covered to discourage popular veneration. He was fastened with irons, but when they tried to nail him as well he told them not to bother. 'The One who gives me strength to endure the flames will also give me strength not to flinch at the stake. There will be no need of nails.'

So Polycarp was bound, like a noble ram, a holy burnt-offering for God. Then he lifted his eyes to heaven and prayed. 'Lord God, Father of your blessed Son Jesus Christ, through whom we have come to know you: you are the God of angels and heavenly powers, and of the whole creation, and you rule over all the righteous ones who dwell with you. Thank you for granting me this day and hour, that I may be counted among your holy martyrs, to share the cup of your Anointed Son, and to rise with them in body and soul to life eternal through your life-giving Spirit. May I be accepted among them today in your presence, a sacrifice rich and acceptable, appointed and foretold by you, who will now bring it to pass. For you are the God of truth in whom there is nothing false. For this, and everything else, I praise and bless you, through our eternal high priest, Jesus Christ, to whom with the Holy Spirit be glory for ever and ever.'

As his 'Amen' soared up, the fire was lit and the flames blazed. But then those present witnessed an amazing sight, which we have been spared to describe to you. The fire took the shape of a hollow room, like a ship's sail filled with the wind, and formed a wall around the figure of the martyr. There he stood in the midst of it, not like a human being in flames, but like a loaf baking in an oven, or a gold or silver ingot being refined in a furnace. And on our nostrils we became aware of a beautiful fragrance, like the odour of incense.

When they realized that his body was not going to be consumed by fire, one of the executors stabbed him with a weapon. As he did so, there was such a rush of blood that it put out the flames, a sight which filled all the spectators with awe. They saw in this the depth of the gulf between those who belong to God and those who do not believe in him. Polycarp, the wonderful martyr for the faith, was surely now in God's hands—bishop of the catholic church in Smyrna, teacher, apostle and prophet. And every word that ever fell from his lips either has had, or will one day have, its fulfilment.

⌘
40: Called to integrity

Many kinds of trouble flow from the love of money. Yet we are all aware that 'we brought nothing into this world, and we can carry nothing out'. Some day we shall live without money, so we should prepare ourselves now by putting God's commandments first and ensuring that integrity, not acquisition, is our watchword whenever money is concerned.

When the elders themselves have done that, we shall be in a position to advise the women in the church about their manner of life. They should be taught Christian attitudes of love and loyalty. Affectionate and true to their husbands, they should be wary about their relationships with other men. Ideally, they should be friendly and warm in an impartial way with everyone, rather than having special male friends—and they should, of course, avoid any hint of impurity.

The Christian widows should be given special support to witness to their faith. Their particular calling is to intercessory prayer for the other members of the church, but this ministry is spoilt if they also spend time spreading gossip and spiteful rumours, stirring up trouble by making unfounded allegations, or trying to acquire money. They should appreciate that they are supported by the sacrificial giving of the other Christians. In that sense, their lives are laid out on the altar, under the scrutiny of God, from whom no secrets can be hidden.

All of us ought to know that God is not mocked. That is why we owe it to ourselves to behave in a manner that conforms to his commands and reflects his glory. Deacons, for instance, must never be open to his reproach, remembering that they are his servants, not the servants of men. They must be utterly self-disciplined, hard-working but sensitive, passing their lives in the spirit of him who came to be 'servant of all'. If we please him in this world, we shall enjoy him in the world that is to come. If we are good citizens of his kingdom now, we shall reign with him in heaven. That is our faith.
POLYCARP OF SMYRNA

⌘

41: Advice to young men and women

The younger men in the church must live lives that are untainted by any kind of sin, with the avoidance of sexual impurity their first concern. They must keep a tight rein on any tendency to lax standards in this area of life. So far as our attitude to the world around us is concerned, it's a good thing to make a clean break with the indulgence of sexual lust. After all, as the apostle Paul says, 'The lusts of the flesh war against the Spirit.' He also warns that no fornicator or sexual pervert will inherit the kingdom of God. We might add, nor will anyone who indulges in a dissolute lifestyle of any kind. Our Christian duty is to give everything of this kind a very wide berth, to steer clear of it. We should cultivate obedience to our bishops and deacons, simply because they represent the word of God and of Christ to us.

And what has been said about young men is also true for young women, of course. In exactly the same way as for the men, Christian women must show that in these matters of sexual purity their consciences are unblemished.
POLYCARP OF SMYRNA

42: Faith, hope and love

To God's Church at Philippi:

It does my heart good to see how the roots of your faith, so firmly planted from the very beginning, are still growing and bearing fruit for Jesus Christ. In him, as you are well aware, endurance went even as far as death on the cross for our sins—but God overcame the grave and raised him to life again. Though you never had the opportunity to see him with your own eyes, yet you believe in him with a glorious joy which is beyond words—a joy many others would be glad to experience. For you know that it is by his grace alone that you are saved, and that it is not of your own doing, but solely by the will of God through the Lord Jesus.

So 'gird up your loins' and serve God in reverence and sincerity. Not that I should be the one to give you this exhortation to the life of holiness. Indeed, I wouldn't have done it if you had not expressly invited me to do so. For I am as far as anyone else from having the wisdom of the blessed apostle Paul. While he was with you in Philippi, he gave the Christians of those days clear and sound instruction in the word of truth, and even after he left you, he continued to send you letters which, properly acted upon, would enable you to make progress in the faith which was brought to you at the beginning. Here was the secret of discipleship. Faith is the mother of us all. Hope follows in her footsteps, while love of God and Christ and neighbour lead the way. If anyone's mind is truly set on these principles, all the demands of holiness will be met, for to possess love is to be beyond the reach of sin.

POLYCARP OF SMYRNA

43: A matter of example

It is a wonderful thought that at this moment friends of ours, people we have known and loved well, are at the side of the Lord in heaven, sharing his joy as once they shared his pains. Their hearts were never wedded to this world and its passing values, but were set on the one who died for us and was also raised from death for us by God.

So take them as examples, just as they took Christ as their example. Hold the faith firmly, as they did. Join together to defend the truth, and love one another as brothers. Indeed, you should make a practice of giving way to one another, certainly not regarding anyone as inferior or beneath your attention. In that way, you will have the spirit of Christ, who never treated any person with anything less than courtesy and love, however poor or sinful or outcast they may have been.

POLYCARP OF SMYRNA

44: The avoidance of anger

I have no doubt that you have a very good grasp of Holy Scripture, and that it presents you with fewer problems than it does me! But doesn't it say there, 'Don't be angry to the point of falling into sin; and don't let the sun set on your wrath'? The happy person is the one who keeps this advice in mind, as I'm sure you do. May the God and Father of our Lord Jesus Christ, and the eternal High Priest Jesus Christ himself, his Son, help you to grow in faith and truth, in a gentleness which never fails and in the avoidance of anger of every kind. May he lead you into patience and tolerance of others, and into a calm and pure way of life. May the Lord grant you, and us, and all those everywhere who believe in him now, and will do in the future ages, a place and an inheritance among his saints.

Pray for all of God's people. But, more than that, pray also for those who rule over you, yes, even those who hate and abuse you. Even pray for those who are enemies of the cross of Christ. In that way, the true fruit of your faith will be plain for all to see, and you will grow into perfection in him.

POLYCARP OF SMYRNA

The Early Church: Reflections

Many of the readings in the rest of this collection reflect the life and character of the Christian churches of the second century. Modern Christians may be surprised to discover that most of the things that disturb and sometimes mar church life today were also present then—these weren't synagogues of angels! But the threat of physical persecution, which was such a feature of their experience, has not overshadowed most Western churches in recent times. That very element may account for the sharpness of some of their judgments on many subjects. The luxury of weighing options and carefully balancing contrary opinions was largely denied them by the awful clarity of the Inquisitor's question, 'Are you a Christian?' or his peremptory command to make sacrifice to Caesar.

Yet aside from that, we may find that we can recognize and respect many enviable virtues in these churches. For one thing, in an age of social stratification, where patricians, merchants, plebs and slaves did not so much belong to different classes as live in different worlds, the Church cut right through the layers. Whatever their faults, its congregations were aware that the Gospel was broad enough to encompass anybody and everybody who believed in Jesus. They were 'all one in Christ Jesus'. They drank from the same cup of blessing. Rich and poor, male and female, free or slave, Roman, Greek, Barbarian or Jew, all were members of the new family of God. Among them were staff of the Emperor's household, alongside slaves from rich merchants' kitchens.

It's safe to say that there had never been anything like it before in human history. It was a unique experiment in social unity of which the Church has cause to be proud, though sometimes individual congregations even in those days did not live up to its highest principles, and the Church of later ages has often and singularly failed to match it.

This was also a community which supported the weak and vulnerable among its members, as we shall read—the elderly and unemployed, orphans and widows. It was a society that resisted the richest and most powerful regime in human history and eventually broke it by its sheer, dogged refusal to compromise its principles. It was a body that met clandestinely, for the most part, and yet managed to share its message of love and forgiveness with any who would listen, and earthed it in the quality of its members' lives.

Those lives were themselves enriched by what they liked to call the 'fellowship'. The Greek word (*koinonia*) conveys a sense of partnership, of people sharing in a common goal. That is the sense in which the New Testament speaks of the Church's 'fellowship'— not a 'feeling', but action and commitment towards agreed ends. This partnership was with one another, of course, but it was also with Christ, a concept most vividly expressed in their central act of worship, the eucharist, in which the broken bread and shared cup were a 'sharing in the body and blood of Christ' (1 Corinthians 10:16).

Their worship seems to have had two elements, the more formal Eucharist, presided over by the bishop or presbyters (elders), and a more informal gathering to hear the Scriptures or letters from church leaders read aloud, together with spontaneous prayer and 'prophecy'. In some places these may have occurred at one and the same time, perhaps early on Sunday morning before the day's work began, or they may have been separated into a larger gathering for communion, involving church members from a fairly wide area, and smaller 'cell' meetings at night in scattered homes across the district. The letter to the Hebrews calls these gatherings 'extra-meetings', literally *epi-synagogues* (Hebrews 10:25).

Preparation for baptism was a long process, involving close examination of the candidate and even exorcism, if it were deemed necessary. Leaders were wary of pagan ideas infiltrating the Church. While children of believers were baptized in the early days, by the middle of the second century this practice was under pressure from an increasing concern about 'post-baptismal sin', which some argued was beyond forgiveness. This led eventually to the postponement of baptism, in many cases almost to a person's deathbed, to guard against even the possibility.

However, as we shall see, during the period of these writings new converts were still baptized, usually at the Easter Eve vigil, after careful preparation, but it is not easy to draw a general rule as to the position of children in the scheme of things. It may be that practice varied in different areas and 'bishoprics'.

This was a Church with many outstanding leaders, some of whose words we still have. But one suspects that its real authority and attractiveness lay in the quality of the lives of its ordinary members, men and women who by their baptism had freely identified themselves with the cause of Christ. Probably the more esoteric theological arguments rehearsed in some of these writings passed as far over the heads of second-century Christians as their 21st-century equivalents do over the heads of congregations today. But they knew 'in whom they had believed', and were persuaded of his abiding presence and love, not only in their own lives, but in the life of the Church to which they gave such unreserved loyalty and commitment.

Epistle to Diognetus

This 'epistle', which is more a treatise than a letter, was written by an anonymous author, probably some time around AD124. Strangely, the manuscript seems to have been lost at some time in those distant days. The Epistle is not mentioned or quoted in any of the writings of the early Fathers of the Church. But a single extant manuscript existed and was discovered in the 16th century. Although there are one or two gaps in this manuscript, and it ends rather abruptly, scholars have agreed in its authenticity as a document of the early Church.

The Epistle is written to counter the great rival religions for Christianity in those early days—Judaism and the Greco-Roman cults—but also to answer a supposed inquirer's request for information about Christian beliefs and practices. In answer, the writer contrasts the stupidity of Greek idol-worship and the alleged barrenness of Jewish legalism with the supernatural nature of the Christian revelation. He backs this up with a unique and beautiful picture of the life of the second-century Christian communities.

45: The difference

It's not possible to tell a Christian from an unbeliever by where he lives, what he wears or the way he dresses. There are no 'Christian towns', there is no 'Christian language'. They eat, sleep and drink in exactly the same way as everyone else. Christians aren't particularly clever or ingenious and they haven't mastered some complicated formula, like the followers of other religions.

But while it's true that they live in cities next door to other people and follow the same pattern of ordinary daily life as they do, in fact they possess a unique citizenship of their own. They are, of course, faithful and loyal citizens of their own lands. But they feel like visitors there. In a strange paradox, every foreign country is their homeland, and their homeland is a foreign country to them.

Destiny has determined that they should live here on earth in the flesh, but they do not live *for* the flesh. Their days are passed on earth, but their real citizenship is in heaven. They obey the laws of the powers that be, but in their own lives they live by a higher law. They show love to everyone—and everyone seems to persecute them. They are constantly misunderstood and mis-represented, yet through their suffering they find life. They are poor, but make many rich. They lack many things, yet have everything that matters in abundance. In their dishonour they are made glorious, in being slandered they are eternally vindicated. They repay insults with blessings and abuse with courtesy. For different reasons, Jews and Greeks may wish them ill, but the fact is that not one of them can offer any good grounds for this hostility.

EPISTLE TO DIOGNETUS

46: The proof about Jesus

When a great king sends an emissary to a rebellious country, you can expect a mission of ruthless power and terror. But when God sent his Son to the rebellious people of earth, he sent him in gentleness and humility, although he was a King sending a son who was also of royal status.

He sent Jesus as God, but he also sent him as a man to men. He sent him on an errand of mercy and persuasion, not of force or coercion. Indeed, coercion is foreign to the nature of God. Jesus came to invite people, not to drive them to repentance. And God's motive for sending him was love, not judgment—though one day he will send him in judgment, and 'who can abide the day of his coming'?

How do we know that he came, the Son of God, the Son of Man? We know as we see the results of that coming: as we see his followers refuse to deny him, even in the face of torture or threats of being flung to wild beasts. We know as we see their numbers increase even as persecution increases—as we see that nothing can conquer their faith in him. Such things are not the work of mortal man. They are evidence of the power of God. They are the visible proofs of the presence of Christ.

EPISTLE TO DIOGNETUS

47: Knowing the Father

In mastering the rudiments of the Christian faith, knowledge of the Father must be the first lesson.

God loved the human race. He created the world for them and it was to them that he ceded care over everything in it. He gave them the gift of reason and understanding, and to them alone he also gave the right to lift up their eyes and see him. He made them in his own image and sent his only Son to them. To those who loved and received him, the Father gave the kingdom of heaven.

Once you have grasped these wonderful truths of the faith, your joy will overflow and love will be kindled in your heart for the one who in this way showed his love for you. And if you love him, you will become an imitator of his own goodness.

It may surprise you that I dare suggest that a mere mortal can imitate the goodness of God himself, but he can, simply because God has willed it to be so. In any case, true joy and happiness is not to be found in dominating one's fellow human beings, or wanting to have greater possessions than others, or acquiring riches, or riding in a roughshod way over those who we feel are 'beneath' us. No one can possibly become an imitator of God by behaving like that, because such behaviour is totally alien to God's nature and character. But if you will shoulder your neighbour's burden, supply his need from your plenty, share the blessings you have received with those in need—then you will become, as it were, 'God' to those who receive the fruits of his love through you.

More than that, when you live in that manner you will discover the true evidence that there is a God in heaven who is at work on earth, and you will be in a position to share with others the joyful mysteries of his love.

EPISTLE TO DIOGNETUS

⌘

48: Knowledge and life

Those who love God truly become another Garden of Eden, a new paradise, and in their lives every kind of good fruit springs up. You will recall that in Eden there were two special trees, the Tree of Knowledge and the Tree of Life. It wasn't the Tree of Knowledge itself that caused the deaths of our first parents, but their wilful disobedience.

After all, God planted those trees. The Bible says, 'In the beginning God planted in the midst of the garden the tree of knowledge and the tree of life'. Surely this indicates that the way to life is through knowledge. It wasn't wrong of Adam and Eve to want knowledge, but it was a deadly sin to disobey God and acquire that knowledge improperly. That was why they were expelled from the garden and lost everything.

In fact, there can be no life at all without knowledge and there can be no reliable knowledge without life, which is why those two trees were planted side by side. Knowledge without life's love is just empty wind, because the person who claims to know, but lacks the life-giving principle of love, in fact knows nothing. Knowledge leads to life and life, spiritual life, leads to knowledge. It is the devil's work to try to keep the two apart.

EPISTLE TO DIOGNETUS

✠

49: A new Eden

Set your heart on life with God and you may confidently expect to sow in hope and gather in a rich harvest of fruit. Your heart will indeed be like the garden of Eden, and by planting the Word of God in this fertile soil, knowledge and life will abound together.

How pleasant this garden will be! Tending the trees and gathering the fruit, your harvest will be pleasing to God—and it will be a harvest which that serpent, the devil, will not be able to spoil.

In that garden, Eve cannot be seduced to disobedience. Knowledge and life flow into it from the Virgin's Son, and from the new Eden flows salvation for those around. Here the evangelist will find his message fresh and new. Here worship is lifted on to a higher plane. Here the Word brings joy and assurance to the believers and God is glorified.

That is the key. Keep knowledge and life *together*, and God will be glorified.

EPISTLE TO DIOGNETUS

Justin Martyr

Justin was born to pagan parents, probably in Palestine, possibly in Shechem. He was converted to Christianity in about AD130. Following this, he taught for a time at Ephesus and later opened a Christian school in Rome. In about AD165 he and some of his associates were denounced as Christians, and when they refused to make sacrifices to the Emperor they were first scourged and then beheaded.

Although he had no real background of scholarship, Justin became the first Christian leader to set about the task of arguing the 'case' for Christianity in the setting of the ancient world. He particularly sought to reconcile the apparently conflicting claims of faith and reason. With great courage, his first 'Apology' was addressed to Emperor Antoninus Pius and his adopted sons, and his second to the Roman Senate itself.

The first Apology defends Christianity as the only truly rational creed and in the course of his arguments he gives a fascinating account of both baptismal and eucharistic ceremonies in the early Church. His second Apology is concerned to rebut specific charges laid against Christian believers. A third book, *Dialogue with Trypho the Jew*, argues the development of the idea of the 'Logos' (the Word) from the God of the Hebrew Scriptures and the place of the Gentiles in the 'new Israel'.

These readings conclude with an account of his examination and martyrdom, which was seen as a 'model' of witness in the contemporary Church.

50: The winning attitude

It is not our task to argue people into the kingdom nor to employ those methods of persuasion favoured by the world. Christ has taught us how to lead people gently and patiently from the love of evil to love of God.

You have probably seen this method in action. Possibly you yourselves were drawn to God in this way. You were violent, perhaps, or inconsistent, or dishonest, or bent on revenge if you were wronged. But you noticed that Christians had a different set of attitudes. Their lives were consistent and reliable, whatever the circumstances. When they were defrauded or wronged, they accepted it with calmness. When you did business with them, you were astonished at their honesty and fair dealing.

And it was probably that which convinced you. The quality of their lives as you saw them as friends, neighbours or colleagues overcame every objection. They had what you most admired and you knew that what they had came from Christ. It was what they did, rather than what they said, that led you to him.

JUSTIN MARTYR: FIRST APOLOGY

51: Living under the vine

We have been completely changed. Formerly our minds were obsessed with violence. Our one ambition was to outdo the other man, whatever the cost. Life was little more than a battlefield for our ambition and greed.

But now the weapons of that 'war' have been transformed. As

the prophet foresaw, we have beaten our swords into ploughshares and the battlefield is now fertile land on which we seek to cultivate love of God, love of neighbour, faith and hope—all of them gifts of the Father through the one who was crucified.

Each of us 'dwells under his own vine', in the words of the Psalmist's vision. Our homes are happy, our marriages secure and our lives contented.

JUSTIN MARTYR: DIALOGUE WITH TRYPHO

⌘

52: Victims of violence

It is true that there is violence in the Christian life, but it is done *to* us, not by us. Because of our faith we are crucified, beheaded, fed to wild beasts or burned in the flames. By these means, some hope to persuade us to deny Christ. They intend to wipe out the Church.

But in fact their persecution has had the opposite effect. Think of the vine. When you 'behead' it, it does not die, but bursts out in other, fruit-bearing branches. That is what happens with us. What others intend for destruction is turned to growth. Unbelievers see this invincible faith and become believers in the Name of Jesus.

After all, he once spoke of this Vine, planted by his Father, rooted in him: it is his people.

JUSTIN MARTYR: DIALOGUE WITH TRYPHO

53: The sign of the cross

The sign of the cross is all around all the time. The mast of a ship carries it—the cross formed by the yardarm is like a symbol of victory as the boat drives ahead through stormy seas. Ploughs and spades bear this cross shape. For that matter, human beings are distinguished from animals by standing upright and being able to extend their arms like a cross.

Even the badges of power in our society express the idea of the cross in powerful symbolism. When the Roman legions march behind their ensigns, they are in fact marching under a cross, and when victory poles are carried, the victory of which they remind us is the victory of the cross.

So, if we wish, we may see the Lord Christ in everything: his victory in every human symbol, his glory in every earthly kingdom, his sign in every heathen inscription.

JUSTIN MARTYR: FIRST APOLOGY

54: The light of the Word

Whatever falsehoods people make up about us, I confess that I not only boast that I am a Christian but try my hardest to live like one. I am not a Christian because Plato is wrong, or because his teaching differs from that of Jesus, but because they are not, and cannot be, identical. That judgment applies to all the other philosophies favoured by people today, whether they be Stoics, poets or historians. We can accept that all of these people speak well and honestly, according to the light they have received from that creative reason which is present in nature itself. But the wisdom which they possess is not infallible and their knowledge is not irrefutable. Nevertheless, whatever they have said which was part of divine truth is also the property of us who are Christians.

The difference lies in this. We worship and submit to the Word which is from the eternal God, the One who is beyond human comprehension. That Word became human for our sake, shared our sufferings and brought us healing. The philosophers and writers saw truth in a fragmentary way, by the glimmers of truth which were within them by nature. That truth which is from God himself is received and believed not according to our intellectual capacity, but solely according to his grace. That is the true 'light of the Word'.

JUSTIN MARTYR: SECOND APOLOGY

⌘

55: Baptism and Eucharist

At our first birth we were born without our own knowledge or choice, simply because our parents came together. The upbringing we had may well have taught us bad habits and even perhaps wicked behaviour. At our second birth, at baptism, we become the children of choice and knowledge. Our sins are formally remitted through our repentance and we are born again of our own decision, in the name of God the Father, and of Jesus Christ, who was crucified under Pontius Pilate, and of the Holy Spirit who spoke of the Saviour through the prophets. In baptism we are washed of our sins and born to a new life, but this only takes place when the candidate has been 'illuminated'—led to the truth by the work and grace of God.

After the new convert, who has been convinced of the truth and assented to it, has been thus washed in baptism, he or she is brought to the place where the Christians are assembled. Here prayers are offered for ourselves and for the newly enlightened disciples, and for all Christ's people in every place, that they may be counted worthy of their calling. At the end of the prayers, we greet each other with the kiss of peace.

At that point, bread and a cup of wine mixed with water are brought to the president of the believers. He takes them and offers up praise and glory to God in the name of the Son and the Spirit, and gives thanks that we are counted worthy to receive these gifts from God. At the end of his thanksgiving, all the people give their assent by saying, 'Amen'.

After that, the people we call 'deacons' give to each one present some of the bread and wine mixed with water over which the thanksgiving has been spoken, and they also carry some away to take to those who are absent.

This food is known among us as 'Eucharist', and no one is allowed to share it except those who believe in the truth of our teaching and have been washed for the remission of sins for a second birth, and are living as Christ has bidden us. This is because we don't receive these things as ordinary bread and wine, but—as we have been taught by the apostles—as the body and blood of Jesus himself, who for our sake became flesh and blood on earth for a time and now nourishes us with this food blessed by the word of prayer.

JUSTIN MARTYR: FIRST APOLOGY

⌘
56: Trial before Rusticus

In AD165, Justin and some of his friends were arrested and brought before the prefect of Rome, Rusticus. This is part of the account of his cross-examination of Justin.

Justin was asked to explain the beliefs of Christians. This was his reply:

We profess concerning the Christian God that he is One, eternal from the beginning, the Creator of all that exists, seen and unseen. We also believe in his Son, our Lord Jesus Christ, whose coming as the Saviour of mankind was foretold by the ancient prophets.

Prefect: You are said to be a learned man. Do you really believe that if you are scourged and beheaded, you will go up to heaven?

Justin: I trust that I shall be given the grace of God to endure such things. I know that for all who so live, grace remains until the end of the world.

Prefect: Do you then think that you will go up to heaven to receive rewards from above?

Justin: I don't *think*, I know, I am fully persuaded.

Prefect: All right. Let's turn to the matter in hand. Will you agree to make sacrifice to the gods?

Justin: No one who is right-minded would turn from the truth to falsehood.

Prefect: If you do not obey, you will be punished without mercy.

Justin: If we are punished for the sake of our Lord Jesus Christ we expect to be saved, for this will give us confidence before the more terrible judgment seat of our Lord and Saviour, on the day that he judges the whole world. You must do what you will. We are Christians and will not offer sacrifices to idols.

At this point Rusticus gave sentence and the martyrs were led away to the customary place and beheaded, 'fulfilling their witness by confessing their Saviour'.

ACTA SANCTI JUSTINI ET SOCIORUM (THE ACTS OF SAINT JUSTIN AND HIS COMPANIONS)

Tertullian

Tertullian was born in Carthage in about AD160 in a pagan family.
He may have trained as a lawyer. After his Christian conversion, he
became a powerful exponent of the faith, vigorously arguing its
cause against the prevailing philosophies, which (unlike Justin) he
rejected totally. Later he joined the Montanists, which was an
apocalyptic movement in the Church, its members looking for
manifestations of the Holy Spirit in the Church's life. It shared
some practices with the modern charismatic movement, but
Tertullian opted to join a rather narrow and rigorist off-shoot of the
movement, which disallowed all second marriages, opposed what
they called 'second repentance' after baptism, regarded the existing
Christian rules on fasting as too lax and forbade Christians to flee
in the face of persecution.

Tertullian is important for his influence on later Christian
thought (especially Augustine of Hippo), particularly in his beliefs
about the fall and original sin. But he is, in his own right, a
powerful advocate of orthodox Christianity and appealed for
toleration of Christians and recognition of their standing in society
as good citizens.

His most important works were *De Praescriptione Haereticorum*
(*Concerning the Rule of the Heretics*); *Apologeticum* (a defence of
Christianity); and *De Animi* (*Concerning the Soul*).

57: How we worship

Christians form a society with a common spiritual energy, a unity of discipline and a hope which we all share. When we come together as a church, we turn to God in prayer, besieging him with our requests like an army storming a citadel. This 'violence' actually pleases him. In our prayers we intercede for emperors, for their ministers and all in authority, for the security of the world and for peace on earth. We also pray that God will postpone the inevitable day of his judgment (to give more people time to repent).

When we meet we also read the Bible, searching for an interpretation of events which helps us to face the future with confidence and seeking to understand their significance. Beyond that, the Holy Scriptures nourish our faith, lift up our hope and confirm our confidence in God. We also find in these words the laws and commands of God.

As well as reading, there is preaching in our gatherings. Sometimes this is intended to encourage and inspire us and sometimes to challenge or rebuke. It carries great weight with us, because we recognize that God sees all our actions and judges them. This earthly judgment is in a way a foretaste of the great judgment which is to come at the end of time. Sometimes, in the light of God's laws, a person will have to be expelled from our community, no longer sharing in our prayers or in holy communion.

Those who preside in our gatherings are called presbyters. They are men of proven character, who have achieved this honour not by bribery but by their Christian character. After all, nothing that belongs to God is up for sale!

TERTULLIAN: APOLOGY

⌘

58: Giving in the church

The church does, of course, have its 'treasury', but it isn't made up of money paid in entrance or membership fees, as if faith could ever be a matter of subscription. Each member brings a financial offering once a month—or more or less often, if they wish, and entirely voluntarily and if they are able to afford it. Let me stress: no one is compelled to give. These are freewill offerings. I suppose you might call them a kind of 'trust fund', setting aside money for holy purposes.

The money given in this way is not spent on banquets or drinking parties, nor to feed the faces of the church leaders. It's used to feed the poor and give them a decent burial; to support orphans who are homeless or without family; to provide pensions for elderly slaves or shipwrecked sailors, or indeed any in need—even prisoners. The only criterion is this, that they should be disciples of God, part of his family.

TERTULLIAN: APOLOGY

⌘

59: True repentance

True repentance involves confession, in which we confess our sin to the Lord, not because he doesn't already know all about it, but because to do so makes us face up to the consequence of our actions. That is the heart of repentance. Confession brings us very low—indeed, often the penitent will clothe himself in sackcloth and ashes and restrict himself for a time to plain and simple food. This is not for the good of his digestion, but of his soul.

What all of this does is to make our act of repentance real and costly. While it brings the penitent low, it also raises him up. While it clothes him with squalor, it actually makes him gloriously clean. While it accuses him of wrongdoing, it also excuses him of its consequence, through the grace of God. While it condemns the sin, it absolves the sinner.*

Let me put it this way. The less excuses you offer for yourself, the more our gracious God will excuse you.

TERTULLIAN: ON REPENTANCE

* After he joined the Montanists, at the end of the second century, Tertullian changed his views on this, allowing no 'second repentance' after the one made at baptism.

⌘

60: The errors of the 'philosophers'

Philosophy is the stuff of the world's wisdom, the impertinent interpreter of the very mind of God himself! You can see that most of the heresies have sprung from such 'philosophy'. I'm thinking of the Platonist, Valentinus, with his 'trinity of man', or Marcion's 'better god'—he was a Stoic. Or take the Epicureans, with their belief that the soul dies. Indeed, almost all the 'philosophers' deny any notion of the resurrection of the body. Zeno seems to teach that all matter is equal to God. In fact, the same questions are constantly addressed over and over again by these heretical philosophers. Where does evil come from? Why does evil exist? What is the purpose and destiny of man? And how can we fulfil it?

What Christians have to assert is this. Athens has nothing to do with Jerusalem—the city of worldly learning with the City of God. What has the Academy to do with the Church? What have heretics to teach Christians? Our knowledge comes from the 'porch of Solomon' (where the apostles taught the first disciples)—and

Solomon called on us to seek the Lord 'in simplicity of heart'. Let's have done with all these futile attempts to produce a Stoic, Platonic or dialectical version of Christianity! Once we possess Christ Jesus, we need no more disputation. The search for wisdom has ended. When we believe, then there is nothing further to add to it. The truth is true, and it is enough.

TERTULLIAN: DE PRAESCRIPTIONE HAERETICORUM

Clement of Alexandria

Born in AD150, Clement became head of the Catechetical School at Alexandria in 190. In contrast to Tertullian, he believed that the great Greek philosophers had value and wisdom, but only in directing seekers to the great source of wisdom, God's 'Word', Jesus. It was felt by some in the Church then, and later, that he leaned rather too far towards the Gnostic view of truth (as an inward 'enlightenment' from the divine) rather than the orthodox view of revelation. For that reason, Pope Clement VIII removed his name from the roll of Christian martyrs. However, it is unlikely that Clement actually joined any of the Gnostic groups and sects, and he was widely respected as an interpreter of Scripture (in the allegorical style of the day) and as a powerful apologist for Christianity.

61: Philosophy as a way to Christ

Philosophy was important in the time before the coming of the Lord to show the Greeks a way of righteousness. But now its value lies in teaching them that all good things, whether they be Greek or Christian, are gifts of providence. In this way they begin to gain the fruit of faith for themselves.

It is plainly true that God is the source of all good things. Some of these are directly his gift—for instance, the old and new covenants of the Scriptures. Others are consequences of his natural ordering of things, and in this category I would put philosophy. Perhaps it was given to the Greek people before the coming of the Lord to fulfil some such function as the Law did for the Hebrew people. That's to say, it 'educated' them, it was a teacher, a guide, preparing them for the 'perfect way of truth' which would be revealed in Christ.

CLEMENT OF ALEXANDRIA: STROMATEIS I

62: The triumph of the gospel

Let's wipe away the fog of ignorance and darkness that obscures our sight, and get a vision of the one true God. Let us worship him with this shout of praise, 'Hail, O Light!' For that is what he is for us who once lay buried in darkness and shrouded with the shadow of death. From him a light shone out, brighter than the sun and sweeter than life itself. That light is life eternal, and those who share in it share in his life. Because of him, night shrinks back from the light and gives place to the 'day of the Lord'. Because of him, the universe has been awakened to life and the setting sun has been turned into a new dawn.

This is what God means by a 'new creation'. The One who circles the universe, the 'sun of righteousness', sheds his light on all without favour, imitating his Father, who 'causes his sun to rise upon all' and sprinkles them all with the dew of truth. He it was who changed the setting into a rising, he it was who crucified death, he it was who snatched mankind from the jaws of destruction and now raises them to heaven. In this work, Jesus is the 'farmer', who reads the signs of the sky, wakens the people to work, and plants what is incorruptible into corruptible soil. This is the soil which will yield the Father's great and divine harvest—a harvest of men and women made anew in his image, with his law written in their minds and on their hearts.

CLEMENT OF ALEXANDRIA: PROTREPTICUS XI

⌘

63: Taught by the Word

There is one style of training appropriate for philosophers, another for athletes, another for orators. In the same way, there is a style of training appropriate for those who would follow Christ. It involves a generous and open character, one suited to the desire for moral beauty which marks his disciples.

For those who are following this regime, there is a kind of dignity, whether it be in their daily conduct, the way they sit at table, the food they choose to eat, the hours they decide to rest, indeed their whole way of life, which marks them out as followers of the Word.

That is why the Saviour is called by that title of 'Word', for he offers to humanity rational remedies which produce healthy sensations and a godly wholeness. Indeed, he devotes himself to their welfare, warning of evil and supplying all the antidotes of salvation to those who are diseased. That is the royal work of God on our behalf.

CLEMENT OF ALEXANDRIA: PAEDOGOGUS (TEACHER) I

Irenaeus

Irenaeus was Bishop of Lyons from about AD178, though he was probably a native of Smyrna and wrote in Greek. However, the text of his main work (*Adversus Omnes Haereses—Against all Heresies*)—exists only in Latin. He is regarded as the first great theologian of the Catholic Church and was a formidable opponent of Gnosticism and also of 'Millenarianism' (the thousand-year period of blessedness associated with the second coming of Christ)—a belief popular in Montanist circles. He was a great advocate of the authority of the apostles and of the Church's role as an instrument of the Holy Spirit. His views helped to form the basis on which the canon of Scripture—the recognition of apostolic writings as 'Scripture'—was decided. He died at the end of the second century.

64: The Spirit in the Church

We receive our faith from the Church, but it is the Spirit of God who daily renews that faith in us. Indeed, the Spirit keeps our faith fresh and young, his precious presence renewing the whole Church. The Spirit is the gift of God to the Church, as vital to its life as the first breath which God once breathed into man's nostrils. The Spirit is the life-giver, breathing life into every member of the Body, the channel through whom we are linked to Christ himself, the assurance of eternal life, the inward witness to the reality of our faith and the ladder by which we can ascend to the presence of God.

'In the Church,' the apostle tells us, 'God set apostles, prophets, teachers' and all the other ministries through whom the Spirit works. Consequently, those who deliberately cut themselves off from the life of the Church, through unbelief or evil, deprive themselves of this priceless gift. For where the Church is, there is the Spirit of God, and where the Spirit of God is, there is the Church and every kind of grace. But the Spirit is truth. So those who do not share in the Spirit are not nourished into life from the breasts of their mother, nor do they drink from the fountain of life which flows from the Body of Christ.

IRENAEUS: BOOK 3

65: Holding fast to the truth

We have the truth which was handed down to us by the apostles, and therefore we should not seek truth from other sources. After all, the apostles, like a rich man depositing his money in a bank, placed into the Church's coffers the richer truth of the gospel, so that whoever wishes to can draw from her the water of life. For that reason, the Church offers us the way into life, and all other 'ways' are bogus—the territory of thieves and robbers. So we should avoid them, holding firmly on to the tradition of the faith which we have been taught in the Church.

If a dispute arises about some matter of doctrine, how should we resolve it? Surely by turning to the witness of the original churches with which the apostles themselves were in constant contact. Shouldn't we want to learn from *them*? The apostles have left us writings, to confirm this evidence. But even if they had not, we should still follow the teaching which the first followers of Christ have passed on to us from them. In this way, those we might call 'barbarians', who can neither read nor write, can still have access to the truth of the gospel and order their beliefs, behaviour and way of life according to the teaching of the apostles.

IRENAEUS: BOOK 3

⌘

66: Four Gospels, one Saviour

It seems fitting that the Church, for whom the gospel is 'the pillar and ground of truth', should have that foundation built on four pillars, which breathe life into the Body. Perhaps that is why the Word, the Creator of all, who sits among the cherubim, should have witness borne to his coming among us under four forms (the four Gospels), bound together by one Spirit. After all, the cherubim had four faces, which were themselves images of the revelation of the Son of God.

The first was like a lion, which symbolizes Christ's royal power and authority. That is Mark. The second was a calf, which denotes his sacrificial and priestly function, to which Luke bears witness.

The third had a human face, testifying that the Son would come among us as a human being—Matthew's witness. And the fourth was an eagle in flight, picturing the gift of the Spirit hovering on outspread wings above the Church, which is John's vision.

The Gospel according to John relates Christ's glorious origins with the Father, declaring in its very first sentence, 'In the beginning was the Word, and the Word was with God, and the Word was God.' This Gospel is full of confident assurance, which matches the portrait of the only Son of God.

Luke's Gospel takes up Christ's priestly character, beginning, as it does, with Zacharias the priest offering sacrifice to God in the Temple. For now the fatted calf was being made ready, to be offered as a sacrifice for the 'younger son', as we are told in this Gospel.*

Matthew relates Christ's human origins, beginning with 'the genealogy of Jesus Christ, the Son of David, the son of Abraham'— and he also tells us much about the birth of Jesus in lowly circumstances, shaping his character as a humble and meek man.

Mark, on the other hand, begins with the ringing voice of the prophet, through whom the Spirit from on high announces the 'Gospel of Jesus Christ' as foretold by Isaiah. His Gospel has wings, though it is both a full and a briefly told narrative.

IRENAEUS: BOOK 3

* See Luke 15:21–24.

⌘

67: The redemption of the body

There are some who despise the revelation of God's truth, rejecting the whole concept of the salvation of the body. Indeed, they maintain that it is incapable of being born again into an incorruptible life. Flesh, they would argue, cannot be saved.

But if this were so, then it also cannot be true that the Lord Jesus redeemed us with his own body and blood, nor that the cup of the Eucharist is a sharing in his blood and the bread which we break a sharing in his body. The truth is, our bodies are saved by his body. The cup of communion is a part of the creation—a part of the physical order of things—but Jesus recognized that it could convey salvation through his blood. The bread which we break is also a part of that created order, yet he affirmed it to be his own body, from which our own bodies and souls would be nourished.

So when the bread and wine receive the Word of God, and the Eucharist becomes the body of Christ, which is received into and nourishes our physical bodies, how can anyone affirm that the flesh is incapable of receiving the gift of God, which is eternal life? If our physical bodies can both receive the body of the Lord *and become part of it*, how can anyone argue that they are incapable of salvation?

IRENAEUS: BOOK 5

The Martyrs of Lyons

It seems appropriate to conclude this collection of writings from the first two centuries of the Church with a moving account of the deaths of a group of martyrs, Christians from Lyons and Vienne in Gaul (modern France). They were arrested and charged simply with being Christians, a charge which brought a mandatory death sentence if proven. The group of people who were arrested included one or two newly baptized Christians, several 'ordinary' church members, men and women, a deacon and their bishop. A few of the local Christians, faced with death in the arena or in various other brutal ways, denied their faith, but the account includes a touching tribute to some of them who repented and went to their deaths alongside the other martyrs.

Martyrdom was the most highly esteemed attainment for Christians in those early centuries. Martyrs—the word literally means 'witness'—had offered the ultimate proof of the reality of their faith. Paradoxically, the more Christians were executed, the more the Church grew, giving rise to that strange saying that 'the blood of the martyrs is the seed of the Church'. A cause worth dying for—and dying in the most degraded and degrading of circumstances—demanded to be taken seriously.

The martyrs of Lyons were executed in AD 177 and the story of the event is recorded by Eusebius in the form of a *Letter to the Churches*. This part of the account tells of the peasant woman Blandina, a local figure, Attalus, and some of those who repented of their earlier denials and were executed with the others.

68: The martyrdom of Attalus and Blandina

Now Blandina, suspended on a stake, was offered as food to the wild animals who were released around her. Just to see her hanging there, in a cross-wise position, earnestly praying aloud, served to strengthen and encourage her fellow Christians. They felt that they could see in her something of the One who was crucified for them and that served to reassure them that those who put their trust in him and suffer for his name have unbroken fellowship with the living God. As it happened, none of the wild beasts even touched her, so she was taken down from the stake and thrown back into prison, there to await further trials at the hands of her captors. She was small, weak and despised, but she had 'put on Christ', her great and invincible Champion, and would in his strength defeat the adversary over many rounds, and finally through it all be crowned with the crown of immortality.

The crowd were now baying for Attalus, who was well known to them. He entered the arena confident, knowing that his conscience was clear, that he had held fast to the Christian way of life and had consistently been a witness among us of the truth. He was led around the amphitheatre behind a board which read, 'This is Attalus the Christian', a sight which seemed to provoke the crowd to a frenzy. However, when the governor found out that he was a Roman citizen, he ordered him to be taken back to the prison, where others also were awaiting the Emperor's decision about their fate.

However, the delay this provided was fruitful, because during that time of waiting the boundless compassion of Christ was revealed. Those who were spiritually as good as dead, having denied the faith, were brought back to life by the witness of the 'living' Christians. Martyrs forgave those who had shrunk from martyrdom. The Church welcomed back those who had appeared to have been still-born. So it was that during this respite the majority of those who had denied were restored to faith, reborn (as it were) and ready to confess Christ. Filled with a new vigour and zeal, they approached the tribunal, asking to be examined afresh by the governor. Truly God takes no delight in the death of a sinner, but is generous towards those who sincerely repent. The Emperor had decreed that those who confessed the faith should be tortured to death, but that any who denied should be set free.

Now, when the governor examined them a second time, they were sentenced in the same way as the others—those who were Roman citizens were beheaded, and the others were sent to the wild beasts. So, confessing Christ, those who had previously denied him were added to the inheritance of the martyrs.

The following day, Attalus was again brought into the arena, because the governor, to please the crowd, had decided to offer him to the wild beasts. When this failed to kill him, every other torture was carried out, including scorching in the 'iron chair', until he achieved martyrdom.

On the final day of the executions, Blandina herself was brought back into the arena, in the company of a young Christian lad called Ponticus, who was about fifteen years old. They had been brought in each day to observe the tortures inflicted on their fellow Christians. The heathen tried to force them to swear by their idols, but they held firm to the end. This infuriated the crowd, who had no compassion either for the youth of Ponticus or Blandina's sex. Instead, they submitted them to every imaginable cruelty, again and again trying to force them to swear. But they failed. Ponticus, encouraged by his sister in the Lord, nobly endured everything they could do to him until he finally 'gave up his spirit'. Blandina died last of all the martyrs, like a mother who had cared for her children and sent them out on a royal pathway before her. Finally she hastened to join them, after enduring scourging, wild beasts, the fire and then being thrown to a bull. When she finally gave up her breath, even the heathen admitted that never in their experience had a woman endured so many terrible sufferings.

FROM EUSEBIUS BOOK 5: 'LETTER TO THE CHURCHES'

For Further Reading

The Early Christian Fathers (a selection from the writings of the
Fathers from St Clement of Rome to St Athanasius),
Henry Bettenson (ed.), OUP.

Early Christian Writings (The Apostolic Fathers),
Maxwell Staniforth (trans.), Penguin Classics.

A New Eusebius (documents from early Church history),
J. Stevenson (ed.), SPCK.

The Christian Testament Since the Bible—Part III (Christian writings
from the times of the apostles to the present day), Mark Booth
(ed.), Firethorn Press.